CONSEQUENCES

Obedience Is Better Than Sacrifice

Yolanda Flournah-Perkins

Faithful Life Publishers
North Fort Myers, FL 33903
FaithfulLifePublishers.com

Consequences ~ Obedience Is Better Than Sacrifice

Copyright © 2012 **Yolanda Flournah-Perkins**
ISBN: 978-0-615-49286-5

Faithful Life Publishers
3335 Galaxy Way
North Fort Myers, FL   33903

www.FaithfulLifePublishers.com
info@FLPublishers.com

VIP Portraits by Cynthia (author picture)
Cynthia Brooks
Contact chopdivabrooks1@hotmail.com

Junky Ave Graphics & Designs (cover design)
Joe McCray "AKA" G.I. DA BOSS
(863) 228-6793

Printed in the United States of America

19 18 17 16 15 14 13 12   1 2 3 4 5 6

DEDICATION

This book is dedicated to my nephews and nieces: James Thicklin, Jr.; Bobby 'BJ' Ray Flournah III; Marcus 'MJ' Lamar Flournah, Jr.; NaTashia Anne Coring; Todd 'TJ' Antonio Flournah, Jr.; Z'Kiria Nell Coring; and Yolanda Terrell Coring. I love you each so dearly and I pray that you will use this book as a reminder to stay obedient to the Word of God.

I declare and decree over your lives now that you become all that God has called you to be. The Word of God says in Deuteronomy 28:13 that you are the head and not the tail and that you are above and not beneath. I cast down anything or anyone that tries to enter into your life and speak things that are contrary to the Word of God. Always remember that God wants you to be obedient, even when it does not feel good; it will be worth it.

Do not be jealous, envy, hateful, mean, rude or disrespectful to people because of something they have that you may want. The Word of God says in Acts 10:34, *God is no respecter of persons.* What He does for one person, He can do for another. There will come a time in your life when you will be living on your own, making your own choices and decisions. Please remember that the choices you make will result in good or bad consequences. Make sure you choose the right one—the one that will leave a positive impact in your life. And regardless of what you decide to grow up and become, I will always love every single one of you!

IN LOVING MEMORY OUR FIRSTBORN SON

DWIGHT "SUNNY BOY" PERKINS

MARCH 19, 2010 – MARCH 19, 2010

Before I formed you in the womb I knew you, before you were born I set you apart...Do not be afraid... for I am with you... declares the Lord. Jeremiah 1:5, 8. Our precious Sunny Boy, while the time you spent in my womb was brief, I will never forget your soft and gentle kicks. You will always have a special place in our hearts and the love we have for you will never end.

Love you always & forever,

Daddy & Mommy

Acknowledgements

And we know that ALL things work together for good to them that love GOD, to them who are the called according to his purpose.

Romans 8:28

Dear God,

Thank you! Thank you! Thank you! The vision to write and the provision to bring forth this book could not have been possible without You. Lord God, your grace and mercy was (and still is) sufficient, and it guided me throughout the entire process. When my enemy tried to attack my mindset and thought process to keep me from writing, You reminded that *No weapon formed against me shall prosper.* When the enemy tried to bring up my past, You reminded in your word, *Therefore if any man be in Christ, he is a new creature: old things are passed away; behold, all things are become new.*

When my enemy wanted me to believe that my life was over, once again I was reminded of your word that *ALL things work together for good to them that love GOD, to them who are the called according to his purpose.* Thank You, God, for I know that my life has purpose , and I know this is true because You said in your Word, *For I know the plans I have for you, declares the LORD, plans to prosper you and not to harm you, plans to give you hope and a future.* Because I know who I am in Christ Jesus, I do not have to hold my down and walk in shame. For God, you have already declared to me *there is no condemnation for those who are in Christ Jesus.*

Thank You, Father, for I am not moved by what people say or how things look in the natural, but I am only moved by what YOUR word says. Thank you for creating in me a new heart, to be able to love my enemies unconditionally, even when my flesh does not want to. Thank You, Father, for reminding me when I am faced with challenges, disappointments and let downs, Your Word says, *I can do all things through Christ which strengthens me.* Even during the time when I questioned why I went through what I did, once again You reminded me in your Word, *But God hath chosen the foolish things of the world to confound the wise; and God hath chosen the weak things of the world to confound the things which are mighty.*

Nevertheless, through all the shame, humiliation and intimidation, I will continue to serve You. Through all the heartaches, job let downs and gossip, I will continue to serve You. With my entire heart, mind, and soul, I will serve You!

To My Loving and Wonderful Husband, Dwight:

Looking back over the last decade of our relationship, all I can say is WOW! Honey, words cannot even begin to describe nor express how much you mean to me. You are truly a man of God. I am so thankful that I was in a position to be found by you!

When we first met in college back in 1999, who (only God) would ever have imagined that we would still be together—

happily married! You are more than my husband—you are my best friend! Even though I made one bad decision in my life, you chose to look above and beyond my faults and focused only on my positive strengths and qualities. Our relationship has truly been tested beyond anyone's wildest imagination and will continue to exemplify that it is because of nobody, but GOD!

I am so in love with you—your behavior, your personality and your character. I remember asking God one night, "Why me? How did I deserve someone as sweet, loving and kind for my husband?" God replied back saying, "Why not you"? The Word of God says in Romans 3:23, *For all have sinned, and come short of the glory of God.*

As we both waited patiently for the arrival of our son (Dwight III), I want to thank you for waiting on me hand and foot around the clock, without uttering a word. For me, being on bed rest for six months was not easy, but I know it was not easy for you either. But nevertheless, what the enemy meant for bad, God blessed us with a beautiful and health baby boy.

Finally, thank you for pushing me to write this book and for not being concerned about what others would say. Thank you for encouraging me to keep writing, when I felt like I could not write anymore. Thank you for reminding me that nobody is perfect, even though some may believe they are. Thank you for wiping my tears and giving me HUGE hugs when every job interview I went on said 'no' even though I was qualified. And thank you for being my backbone and support through it all!

I look forward to spending the rest of my life with you and enjoying our new title— parents. I love you, Baby!

To My Son, Dwight III:

Before I formed you in the womb I knew you, before you were born I set you apart: I appointed you as a prophet to the nations.

Jeremiah 1:5

Lil Dwight, you have no idea how the enemy tried to attack my body immediately after your father and I learned that we were pregnant. When I began writing this book, I would bounce ideas back and forth to you, only to feel your hard kicks and punches against my belly. I never realized how different my outer body appearance would change in nine months, but it did. Even though we endured several losses and experienced hurt and pain, to feel you growing inside me was worth every minute. And if I had to do it all over again, I would not even hesitate. You have truly been a blessing to me and have taught me a valuable lesson—to have patience! I look forward to watching you grow and be all that God will call you to be. You are and will always be MY LITTLE WARRIOR!

To My Spiritual Parents: Pastor Rob and Roxanne King of Disciples of Christ Development Center (DOC):

The two of you have made such a profound and positive impact in my life. Not only are you inspirational, but you are encouraging and motivating. It was not accident or coincidence that I happened to be looking for a hair stylist and church at the same time, but that is how God had it orchestrated. God has called you both to a foreign land in Lehigh Acres to pastor a prosperous church. It has been such a blessing to be under the spiritual leadership and guidance of your teaching at DOC. In addition to being great pastors, you both are wonderful mentors, motivational speakers and positive role models. Thank you for speaking positively in my life and the life of my family. Thank you for showing me how to have Heaven on Earth! FROM BED REST TO BOOK BEST!!

To My Immediate Family:

Mom, Dad, Vince, Tracy, Renee, Dwight Sr., Bobby Jr., Christine, Marcus, Helenia, Todd, Lucy, Natasha, Grandma Daisy, Virgil, Raymond, Uncle Michael, Cherill, Mikey, Uncle Elmer, Sky, Tyrell, Boss, Eugene, Evans, John, Lulu, Curtis, Shawanda, CJ, Daniel, Naji, Tyrone, Auntie Nita, Briana, Justin, Daryl, Grandma Lois, Auntie Mickey, Uncle Haley, Junior, Sonya, Norris, Nikki, Deja and M.B – Thank you all for your love and support!

Rest In Peace—Auntie Pat, Auntie Skeeta, Auntie Mary and Sonny "Yaya" Porter—You all may be gone, but you will never be forgotten. You all are truly missed!

A Special Thank You:

While there have been so many people who have entered into my life, it is impossible for me to name each and every single one of you all—so I am thanking you now.

However, there are just a few people I must recognize: Mrs. Kimberly Scruggs-Tobias, Dr. Mia German, Mrs. Tisha Moorer, Mrs. Dessie Thomas, Mrs. Jocelyn Brown-Lewis, Mrs. Doris Strong, Mrs. Shanita Hardy, Mrs. Damita Smith-Barnes, Ms. Joan Clarke, Ms. Melissa Gonzalez, Ms. Monshay Gibbs, Minister Helen, Ms. Letha James, Mrs. Elaina Bolar, Minister Helen, Mrs. Tasheekia Perry, Ms. Quoya Moore, Mrs. Ozella Ward, and last but certainly not least, my best friend, Natasha Jackson.

To My Readers:

I would like to personally thank each and every one of you for purchasing and reading this book. This book was written based on my past life experiences. I hope it will serve as a lesson for those who read it and follow the main character. It is also my desire that as you read this book you will think about the choices you make in life—and the consequences that subsequently could follow.

There are two wise sayings that I want you to keep in mind as you read this book: *A hard head makes a soft behind* and *You make your bed hard, you lie in it.* Some choices we make in life are a result of our own actions and disobedience. However, if you could learn from the mistakes of others, then do so. Life will present you with plenty of options, but it is up to you to choose the right one. Choosing the wrong option could potentially cause you to face prison or death. Choosing the right decision can lead you to eternal life. No one is perfect but we should all strive for perfection.

The imperfections and flaws of the character were written so that you would examine and/or reexamine your life. If you are in situation where you feel that your past, regardless of how big or small, is keeping you from achieving your dreams—the devil is liar! Yes, facing your past may not feel good and probably will hurt, but I am here to tell you that it will be okay. Own up to your mistakes, embrace your past and push through your obstacles. No situation is too big or small for God to handle. I can assure you that if you change your mind set, you will change your life! Do not allow the enemy (friends, family, etc.) to enter into your thought realm and make you think that you are not worthy of having or living a better life. There will come a point in your life where you will say to yourself, "If it is to be, it is up to me!" What move are you planning to make with your life!

WHEN YOUR HEART IS RIGHT WITH GOD AND YOUR DESIRE IS TO PLEASE GOD, GOD IS OBLIGATED TO PLACE YOU IN THE COMPANY OF THE PEOPLE YOU NEED TO KNOW THAT IS CRITICAL TO YOUR SUCCESS AND DESTINY IN LIFE.

Pastor Robert King Jr.
Disciples of Christ Development Center
Lehigh Acres, Florida

Chapter 1

IN THE BEGINNING

"Here's the deal, Lauren. If you plead guilty, I'll see if I can get the prosecutor to drop one of the charges. You're facing ten years alone on just one of your charges. Unless you plead guilty you'll be serving some serious hard time. Lauren! Lauren! Do you hear me? Are you listening to me?"

"Yes, yes, I am!" Lauren could not believe the words coming out of her attorney's mouth. *Prison! Really!* Not Lauren. This was something that was supposed to happen to somebody else, not her.

Lauren was in her attorney's office discussing possible avenues for her defense. According to him, Lauren was facing some serious allegations that could potentially put her in prison for a very long time. There were piles and piles of brown folders spread all over his conference room table. She could not believe that all those files were for her. He was advising her to plead guilty, because if her case went to trial the prosecutors would surely go after her with the most severe and swift punishment possible.

"Lauren, it would be very wise for you to consider a plea bargain to either one or both of the charges against you. You don't want to waste the government's time and energy in preparing for a trial that does not look promising for you."

She had no idea what to do. Lauren didn't want to plead guilty because she didn't think her crime was that bad. After all, she hadn't killed anyone. And if she did plead guilty, what would everyone think about her?

Her attorney continued, "Lauren, I understand that this is a lot for you take in, but you're going to have to make a decision sooner or later. I'll be in touch with you once I hear back from the prosecutors on the pending charges against you."

Lauren thanked him as she exited his office. She had no idea of the challenges that were ahead of her!

As she walked back to the parking garage, she thought about the last few weeks of her life and how everything had changed. Now she just wanted to get away and hide. *Thank God for tinted windows,* Lauren thought as she drove out of the parking garage and away from attorney's office. She felt as though everyone in Orlando was staring at her. She had no place to go and she didn't want to go back home, even though her mom and sister had come up to attend her arraignment following her arrest. She would feel a lot safer once she got back to her own apartment.

As she was leaving downtown Orlando, Lauren wondered where her boyfriend was at and what he was doing. She tried to call him before going to see her attorney, but he did not answer. *He's probably in class or at practice,* she thought.

As she drove on to her apartment off of Curry Ford Road, she felt as though every Tom, Dick, Larry, and Moe was staring at her. *Could it really be? Could all these people possibly know who I am and know what kind of car I drive?* Lauren did not realize how nervous she was. She felt as though a tidal wave had come through her life and swept her away—she was barely holding on with a life preserver. As she pulled into the parking lot, she noticed a few of the residents walking across it. She decided to sit in her car and wait for awhile before she got out. She wanted to make sure that nobody saw her go into her apartment.

Once she got into her apartment, she checked her phone to see if she had missed a call from Jason, but she hadn't. "I wonder why Jason isn't answering any of my call," she said as she picked up the phone and tried calling him again—five more times. Each time she left a message and each message was uglier than the one before. "He knows it's me calling and he's not answering! I need to see him right now." Lauren was upset.

It had been nearly a day since she had eaten, but Lauren wasn't hungry. She grabbed a drink from the kitchen and walked back to her bedroom. Lying on the bed, she started thinking about things. She wondered what her next move would be and thought about the possibility of going to prison. *Would a judge really convict me and find me guilty? Surely, there's no way a small town country girl like me would end up in prison. I'm not a bad person. Sure, I've made a mistake or two in my life, but nothing that would warrant time in prison. There are a lot of other people out there doing wrong all the time, and they want to make me out to be the bad guy. I'll kill myself before I'll go to prison!*

Lauren continued thinking about the last few weeks of her life and how everything had turned inside out. What was she going to do about this problem? How could she make it all go away? Why did she allow herself to get caught up in this situation? What in the world was she going to do? Lauren moved to Orlando after graduating from high school to attend college, not to go to prison. She was scared and had every reason to be. She was only 22 years old and had a whole lot of life ahead of her—going to prison for ten years was not in her plan.

"Dear God, if you can hear me now, please make this horrible feeling and dream go away!" she cried. But Lauren knew deep down inside that this feeling would not be leaving her anytime soon. She didn't have anyone she could talk to and she didn't trust anyone. More or less, she did not believe that she would even live long enough to deal with her consequences—there was no way she would ever go to any prison and that was that!

While still waiting to hear from Jason, she began to entertain thoughts of suicide. She had never attempted it before, but had heard of people doing it. *I could jump from the third floor of my building or maybe I could hang myself from the ceiling with a rope.* She continued to consider various ways she could commit suicide, to get rid of the situation she was facing. She had heard people say that God doesn't forgive anyone if they commit suicide, but she was positive He would understand her situation and she would not end up in hell. *I mean, they say God sits high and looks low. If that is the case, then He sees the situation I'm in. I'm sure He would forgive me.*

Lauren knew that a decision had to be made soon, because her attorney had to notify the prosecutors. *Well, I do know one thing, if God is a forgiving God, He will have no choice but to forgive me; then I will go to heaven. Besides, who wants to be here on this earth anyway, with the way things are going?*

Lying on her bed, Lauren's mind began to wander. *How can I escape this horrible dream without ever being caught?* Right now in her mind, suicide was sounding pretty sweet. If she committed suicide, how would the prosecutors be able to charge her with the crimes she had committed? She would be dead! Yes, her family would be sad, but they would get over it as time went on. People lose loved ones all the time to suicide, but life continues—what would make her family any different. Besides, no one in Orlando really knew who she was anyway. More importantly, the world would be a much better place without her. She was just one of thousands of people living in this city, so she was pretty sure she would not be missed.

Then Lauren thought about Jason. *Would he miss me?* She reasoned that he probably would miss her a little, but he had his whole life ahead of him. He was attending the university in Orlando on a basketball scholarship and would eventually go on to the big league—which was something he talked about constantly. She knew that he was only with her because she allowed his unfaithful behavior. But as crazy as it may seem, she was okay with it. She knew he cheated on her, but felt she had no other choice but to accept his infidelity—after all, he was an athlete. Every female on campus was attracted to him, including Lauren. Her thoughts then went back to when they first met.

Chapter 2

LAUREN MEETS JASON

Lauren had just returned to the United States after living in Barcelona, Spain for two years. Her first night back she got a welcome call from Maria, a good friend of hers. Lauren had kept in touch with Maria while living in Spain and was happy to know that her friend had relocated to Orlando. "Welcome home, Lauren! How does it feel to be back in the States?" Lauren was excited to be home, but would always consider Spain her home away from home. Maria and another friend of hers were going out for a night on the town and wanted Lauren to tag along.

"Well, I want you to get dressed. One of my girlfriends and I are going to come through and scoop you up for a night out. There's a party going on and there will be some hot guys there. We must be in attendance!" Maria always had something going on. She knew exactly what to say to convince Lauren to come along and she was not about to resist!

Since Lauren had just got to town, she still had a lot of unpacking to do; so she decided to go out and buy herself an outfit for the party. At 8:30 that evening Maria called to let her know they were downstairs waiting on her in the parking lot. Lauren told her that she would be down in a few seconds and hung up the phone. *Just a little more touching up and I'm all set to go.* Lauren was always somewhat insecure about the way she looked and dressed and she wanted to make sure she was on point for that night. Poised, primed, and propped, Lauren was ready to go out and enjoy the night life in Orlando.

Lauren hopped in the back seat of a two door car. Maria introduced her to Tanya, a girl that lived in her apartment complex. Tanya was from south Florida and seemed like a pretty cool person. After the introductions Tanya pulled out of Lauren's parking lot and they were ready to hit the city. Sitting in the back seat, Lauren couldn't see much, but she was so glad that this night did not consist of walking. She had on some high heel boots and her feet were already hurting.

The first stop they made was to the off-campus housing area where the basketball players at the university lived. As they drove through the parking lot, Tanya thought she recognized one of the guys standing outside the building. They started whistling for her to stop, so she did just that. The guys noticed a car with females inside and naturally wanted to see what the ladies looked like. They approached the driver's side where Tanya was sitting and began to engage in conversation. One of the guys wanted to see who else was in the car, so he walked around to the passenger side where Maria was sitting and asked her name. After telling him, Maria asked his name—it was Jason.

Jason wasn't Maria's type so she was not interested in him at all. Then Jason peered inside the car to see who was sitting in the back seat and started a conversation with Lauren. Lauren was very interested. He asked her if she had a man and she told him no. She asked him if he had a girlfriend and he replied, "No, I do not. I'm single and I'm looking for me a woman!" So Lauren asked Jason for his number and he said, "No, but you can give me yours." And that is exactly what Lauren did. She gave Jason her phone number and thought to herself how fine this guy was. It had to be a dream, because in reality fine men did not ask for her number. And now three years later, they were still together.

Lauren's thoughts were suddenly interrupted by the opening of her room door—it was Jason! She stood up and gave him a hug and a kiss—something she always did when he came over. She was so happy to see him and to be in his arms. He had a way of making her feel safe and protected.

"Look, we need to talk. I have no idea what's going on, but you and I need to talk. I got a call today saying that you were arrested and that investigators were here questioning you about some incident that I have no clue about. What's going on, Lauren?" Although she had no idea who told him, she knew it was time to tell him the truth about what happened; but she also knew the minute she told him everything, he would leave her. Jason continued, "Look, let me go take a shower and get settled down. Then you and I will talk."

When Jason walked out of the room, Lauren thought about her behavior and what she had done. Every decision she had made up to this point was for him and for him only. She didn't want him to leave her, so she did whatever she could do to keep him, even if that meant engaging in illegal criminal activity. She knew that he would love her, if he gave her a chance.

Lauren wasn't the prettiest girl in Orlando, but she was almost certain that material things would keep Jason coming back. No one had ever told her anything different regarding relationships, so she did what she thought was right to keep her man. She thought he was happy—each time she bought him something or gave him money, he always seemed so happy. She was sure it would keep her ahead of all the other females on campus. But why? Why did she feel this way about him?

Jason was a very handsome guy. He stood about six feet four and weighed around 260 pounds. His physique was toned in every way possible. His hair was a clean cut low shave which complemented the dimples in his cheeks when he smiled. He had the most beautiful light colored hazel eyes she had ever seen. She initially thought they were contacts, but soon realized they were his natural eye color. The one thing she loved about him the most, though, was how secure and protected he made her feel. She had never been attracted to tall guys because she was short, but loved the fact that he was almost two feet taller than her.

Lauren would do almost anything for this guy, which is why she was in the predicament that she was in. When Jason got out of the shower, he walked into the kitchen to pour himself something to drink. He practically lived there with Lauren—even though he had a place on campus, he hardly ever stayed there. He and Lauren were a couple 75% of the time; the other 25% of the time, he was someone else's man. Lauren was okay with that and knew what she was getting herself into—she just didn't think she would ever get caught up.

The first thing Jason wanted to know was why police investigators were in her apartment. Lauren dreaded this conversation and wanted it to be over before it even started. Why was she able to talk so openly to a bunch of complete strangers, but afraid to talk to Jason. As they sat there in complete silence, staring at each other, Lauren began to cry. "They said I am going to prison, Jason. I can't go to prison!"

Jason didn't know what to do. He had no idea how much trouble Lauren was in. The one thing he did know was that he was not going to stay at her apartment that night. He knew he couldn't leave her by herself, so he suggested that she stay at his dorm for the night and they would figure the rest out later. In the meantime, he had to find out exactly what was going on and why there were police investigators in her apartment. And, even more importantly, now he realized why he had been visited by two police investigators six months earlier.

Chapter 3

Jason's Meeting in the Coach's Office

Approximately six months prior, Jason was in the locker room getting ready for basketball practice when Coach Kilsner approached him. "Jason, I need to see you in my office." He didn't figure it was anything and therefore he didn't worry. He was never late for practice, he was always on time, and he never allowed himself to get in any situation that would bring about negativity. His main purpose for being at the university was to play basketball with hopes of going on to play in the National Basketball League.

As Jason walked into the coach's office, he noticed there were two police officers sitting down. When he entered the female officer stood up and introduced herself as Detective Jasmine Lipzone and the other officer as Detective Michael Stonecole. They wanted to speak with him about a possible theft that happened near the university campus regarding missing parking decals.

Apparently, one of Jason's teammates, whom they called Charlie D, was running late for class and parked in the wrong parking area. When the university parking patrol went to issue the ticket, they discovered that the decal he was using had been reported stolen, so the vehicle was towed. When Charlie D went to pay to have his car taken out of impound, the towing company would not release his car. Instead, they told him that he must contact the University Police Department.

When he called the University Police Department, they informed him that he would have to come on campus and speak with an officer. When he arrived back on campus and reported to the University Police, they wanted to know how he ended up with the stolen parking decal. Apparently there had been repeated complaints, coming from a certain off-campus university housing complex, that parking decals were missing. After a lengthy investigation with the University Parking Services Department, it was determined that there was a possible theft going on.

Charlie D was already on probation for an unrelated charge, so there was no way he was going to take the rap for another person and end up back in jail. Without further hesitation, he informed the campus police that his teammate, Jason, gave him the parking decal. They asked him if he knew who gave Jason the decal. He said he thought Jason got it from his girlfriend, Lauren, who worked at one of the apartment complexes near the university. Upon hearing that information, the investigators knew that their suspicions were right about the possible theft allegations coming from the off-campus apartment complex.

Detective Lipzoni informed Jason that she wanted to ask him a couple of questions regarding a parking decal that was reported lost from a student. They explained the situation with Charlie D from a few weeks earlier and wanted to know how he got the parking decal. Jason knew that he got it from Lauren, but he didn't want to throw her under the bus—he wasn't that kind of guy. At the same time, he could not believe that his own teammate would rat him out like that. He vowed he would never trust him or any of those guys again. "I found it on the side of the road near the woods when I was leaving my girlfriend's apartment," he answered.

Jason knew that if he told the detectives that Lauren gave him the decal, she would get in a lot of trouble and possibly lose her job. This way, his girlfriend was protected and there was no other proof linking her it. And his teammate—well, he was a two-time convicted felon on probation. He was sure they would not believe a convicted felon over him. But as he was looking at Detective Lipzoni, there was something about her eyes that told him she didn't believe a word he was saying. It was as if she knew he was lying and she enjoyed every minute of it. Detective Stonecole didn't say much. He seemed more like the note taker, jotting down everything that came out of Jason's mouth.

Jason could feel the heat and pressure rising on his shoulders as his legs began to shake and wobble. He knew that if he stood up, he would probably fall right down to the floor. All he wanted was for this to be over. And shouldn't he have an attorney present if they were questioning him about a possible theft? But his coach was present in the office, so he figured it was all good.

"Jason, we are currently investigating several incidents over at the Kings Krossing apartment complex. Can you think of any reason why someone would toss a perfectly good parking decal away, when the cost of them is not cheap?" Jason had no idea where this lady was going with her questioning. All he knew is that he wanted this to be over. "Jason, let me be frank with you. We are investigating a few things over at the complex where your girlfriend works. We will get to the bottom of this. If it turns out that you are involved, along with your girlfriend, you can kiss your basketball career goodbye!"

Jason could not believe what he was hearing from Detective Lipzoni. All he knew was that Lauren gave him several parking decals, which he had given to some of his teammates. He had no idea what other investigation this lady could be referring to. "Jason, my suggestion to you is to take a good long look at your girlfriend. You may even want to take a picture of her face, because there is a huge possibility that she is the main person of interest in this investigation. If our suspicion is right, she could be going away for a long, long, long time."

Coach Kilsner then asked Jason if he had any known knowledge about any of the incidents that were happening at the apartment complex, but he did not. In fact, Jason really had no clue just how much trouble Lauren was really in.

Chapter 4

LAUREN'S FIRST THOUGHT OF SUICIDE

"Lauren, we need to talk about what's going on." But Lauren didn't want to talk to Jason or anybody else for that matter. She wanted all this madness to go away, as if it never happened. She wasn't sure if she was embarrassed or ashamed to divulge everything to Jason, like she had done with the police investigators. She didn't want to tell him everything, because she was afraid of losing him. She had worked so hard at this relationship and knew that once he found out what she had done that he would be gone—leaving her by herself.

She didn't mean for him to get dragged into her mess, but she was doing it all for him. She was in love with him and that's all that mattered. She desperately wanted him to hold her real tight and tell her that everything was going to be okay, but he didn't. Instead, he was staring at her like he knew her lies had caught up with her. He was furious with her, because somehow he had become involved in a scheme he had no idea about.

Jason knew that Lauren was insecure about how she looked and the way she looked. She needed him to be there for her and to stand by her side, but Jason was adamant about finding out what was going on. Whether the discussion took place at her apartment or his dorm room, he had to know what happened. They decided to leave her apartment and head back to his. As Lauren stared into Jason's hazel colored eyes she knew that he was upset. He was the last person she wanted to hurt. She knew that she would eventually have to deal with the consequences of her actions, but she never thought she could lose her freedom.

Before they left her apartment Lauren decided she would take a quick shower. While in the bathroom she started crying. She cried softly, because she did not want Jason to hear her. Deep down inside she was hurting with fear—she was petrified. She knew the decisions she made had consequences attached and there was nothing she could do about it. As she stepped in the shower her legs shook like leaves on a tree. She was exhausted mentally and physically, and had a headache the size of Texas. She had never felt so alone or so afraid before in all her life. *There is no way I am going to prison. Not today, not tomorrow, not ever will I step foot into a prison. I will kill myself before I get put in prison.* "Over my dead body, and I mean that," Yolanda cried out loud, while in the shower.

To put it simply, Lauren was scared. Her mother always told her that *if you make your bed hard you will have to lie in it.* Could this really be it? Could she really be getting ready to lie in her bed for the poor choices and stupid decisions she had made a year and a half earlier. She could not believe how foolish and mindless she had been. One of the female investigators even commented on the stupidity and senselessness of her choices. She told Lauren that she was a horrible person and deserved everything that was coming to her.

She stood in the shower feeling the warm water running all over her body. Her muscles were sore and her bones were aching. Her neck felt as if someone had taken a pile of rocks and tied them around it. She could visibly see her hands and legs shaking and she felt numb. She wanted to get away from all the heartache and pain, but she couldn't. She began to think about suicide again and how it would relieve her from all the embarrassment she was experiencing. *If only I could drown myself in the water while taking a shower.*

Lauren knew the only way to follow through with a suicide attempt would either be with a gun or jumping off a place; she even considered getting into her car, jumping on the expressway or interstate, and running her car directly into oncoming traffic. *That would be a sure way to end this tragic nightmare.* The attention she was getting from the media was too much and she could not handle it. There was no way she would be able to endure the outcome of her choices and embrace the consequences of her actions—no way at all. Then she suddenly remembered Jason's gun.

A few months ago Jason bought a gun. He and some of his friends would go to the local gun range to shoot. He had plenty of bullets because he went as often as time would permit. As a matter of fact, he and a few of his friends went to the gun range just a few days earlier. *That's it. Problem solved. I'll wait until we get back to his place and then do it!* Lauren had it all figured out. *Let's see who gets the last laugh now!* She decided that when they got to his place, she would go ahead and tell him everything. Then, when he woke up the next morning, she would be dead—and he would be left with the lie she had been telling him.

Lauren finished her shower and got dressed. She even seemed to have a little bit more spunk in her step, which Jason noticed right away. "Your shower was okay?" he asked coldly. "Yup," she replied. She could feel Jason eyeing her up and down. She wanted to run over and give him a hug and kiss, but she knew it wasn't the place and definitely not the time for that. The negative tension in the room made Lauren very uncomfortable and uneasy. But she understood why he was upset and knew he had every right to be. If only she had told him the truth; maybe, just maybe, he would have liked her for who she was.

While getting dressed, Lauren noticed how awful her room looked. When the investigators approached her outside of her apartment and identified who they were, she gave them full permission to go through everything—a mistake she would never make again. They didn't even have a search warrant. They just flashed their badges and Lauren knew they were there for her. *How could I be so stupid!* Lauren did not know it at the time, but she could have asked them to show her a warrant. But they were threatening her by telling her that if she didn't comply, they would take her to jail and she would be all over the news. Jail was the last place she wanted to be and she definitely did not want to be on the news. Needless to say, her room was a complete disaster!

The investigators went through her room and tore it up like a hurricane. There were papers everywhere and clothes all over the place. They ripped off her bed linens and flipped her mattress over near her nightstand. They went through her purses, book bags, text books, and folders. They even brought in boxes to carry away information that she voluntarily allowed them to take. The more and more she thought about it—if anyone convicted her, she did it herself.

Chapter 5

LAUREN'S FAMILY BACKGROUND

Lauren and her younger sister, Lisa, grew up in a small suburban town near north Florida. Her parents divorced when she was just five and her sister was two. They were raised by their mother, Sheila, who worked full time as a bakery manager. Lauren was a very smart and bright student in school who was fascinated with mystery novels and love poems. She kept a diary from the time she was in fifth grade and had a secret passion for writing. In her spare time she enjoyed playing basketball and tennis, something she did very well. She was well known in her community and throughout the school system.

Because Sheila was a single mother of two, it was very hard for her to do things with her kids and take them places. Lauren's mom worked on Sundays, so they seldom went to church. If Lauren or her sister went, it was because a friend from school invited them; but attending church on a regular basis was not something that they did.

All in all Lauren was an energetic, outgoing girl with a wonderful personality and promising future. While in high school her Spanish teacher, Mrs. Friendly, encouraged her to get involved with a local traveling club, which provided opportunities to travel to other countries. Lauren had never been outside the state of Florida, so visiting another country was a big deal! Lauren did not travel much, but she watched a lot of television and knew that there were places out there for her to visit. There was nothing wrong with where she lived, she just felt that there was more to offer in life— more places to visit and more things to see and do. She planned on enlisting in the military following graduation, but changed her mind following a conversation with a family member. She later decided she would become an airline stewardess, a rewarding field that would allow her to travel all over the world.

At Lauren's first travel club meeting, she was invited to participate in a yearlong study abroad program, where she would serve as an ambassador for her local club. She knew that her mother would not like the idea, so she devised a plan to trick her mom in the conversation about the trip.

Lauren recalled the conversation like it was yesterday. "Mama, guess what? The local travel club I joined is sponsoring high school students around the country to participate in a study abroad program. All I have to do is buy a passport and the club pays for the airline ticket. You would just have to send me money so I could buy the things I need and nothing else." Her mother was in the kitchen cooking dinner. She was tired from standing on her feet all day. The last thing she wanted to hear was Lauren talking about a trip and needing money. But Lauren stood in the kitchen right along with her mother, waiting patiently for her response.

"No, Ma'am. I'm not going to let you go to another country and live with complete strangers that we don't know. Girl, are you crazy?" Lauren knew that her mom would not be easily convinced, so she kept asking her over and over again. Lauren was notorious for repeating questions and knew just how far she could push her mom. "Ma, please let me go. Veronica's parents are letting her go. Please Ma, please let me go!"

Lauren knew that she was getting on her mother's last nerve. As a single parent raising two girls, Sheila knew there was no extra money to spend on any trip. "Listen to me, Lauren. You are not going and that is the end of the conversation. That's it. Don't ask me about this again. Do you hear me? Do you hear me?" Lauren nodded her head and knew that was the end of the conversation.

The next day in class Mrs. Friendly approached Lauren about the travel club meeting and asked if she would be participating in the study abroad exchange program. Lauren could not tell her that her mother had already said *no,* so she smiled and said, "Yes, Ma'am." Yes, Lauren lied to her teacher, but it was not so bad that anyone would be hurt by it. Lauren's mom was well known at the school and she didn't want anyone to think that her mom would disagree with her living abroad.

Lauren had no idea how she would convince her mother to complete the application for studying and traveling abroad when she had already said no. So, after careful thinking and much consideration, she decided to fill out the application herself and sign it with her mom's signature. Signing her mom's name was not a big deal anyway; after all, she had signed her mom's name on other school documents for her and her sister when her mom was not available.

The following day Lauren handed the completed application back to Mrs. Friendly. "Which country did you select, Lauren?" she asked while placing the application packet in her bag? "I chose Barcelona, Spain. Maybe I can learn how to speak Spanish in one year!" Lauren said, as she left the classroom. Mrs. Friendly had no idea that Lauren had forged her mother's signature on the documents. She was going to be in some serious trouble when her mother found out.

A week or so later while Sheila was at work, a coworker came up to the bakery counter and congratulated her on Lauren's upcoming international trip. Sheila had no idea what her coworker was talking about. "Sheila, your daughter is on the front page of the local paper about her upcoming trip to Spain for a year! That is really brave of you to let her go live with complete strangers. There is no way I would let my kids go to another country."

Sheila knew nothing about Lauren going to Spain. What she recalled from their conversation the other night was that Lauren was not going to any country outside of the United States of America. She was furious. Lauren had completely disobeyed her. Sheila had to find one of those newspapers to see exactly what her daughter had done. On her afternoon break, she found a newspaper and went into the employee break room to read it. As she sat down she immediately saw her daughter on the front page shaking the hand of the president of the local travel club in their town with a big smile on her face. *I wonder how big her smile will be when I tell her she will not be going. I can't believe this child went behind my back and did what I told her not to do. I'm going to kill her!*

As Sheila finished her lunch, a few more of her coworkers came to congratulate her on Lauren's upcoming travel to another country. Her daughter would be the first in the community to participate in a travel abroad program. The article said that the trip would open her up to another culture, another way of life, and the possibility of learning how to speak another language—specifically Spanish. Sheila's coworkers felt that Lauren was setting a positive example that would surely be followed by other young kids in the community. As Sheila continued to receive congratulations from her coworkers, she wondered if she was mad at her daughter for wanting to go on the trip or if she was mad at her daughter for being disobedient.

As Sheila was leaving work for the day she ran into a local prominent leader of the community. Dr. Maurice Cummings was a local community activist in the town. He was known for seeking justice in unjust places. He approached Sheila and expressed how wonderful it was that Lauren would be embarking on a new challenge and opportunity in life. He shared his sincere wishes and commended Sheila on the wonderful job she was doing is raising both Lauren and Lisa. He was proud of Lauren for stepping outside the box and outside of her comfort zone.

While getting into her car, Sheila could not help but have a huge smile on her face. Her daughter was getting ready to travel to another country and experience another culture—something she was never exposed to as a young girl. She was excited and happy for Lauren and knew that she deserved this opportunity, just as much as any other high school student that would be going. She would make sure that Lauren was prepared for her trip to Spain, but there was another conversation to have with her first. *She disobeyed me and went behind my back, because of that she will face consequences for her actions.*

Sheila knew that her daughter enjoyed talking on the phone—that would be her punishment, no phone for a week. *Would that really serve as a punishment for her when she will still end up going to Spain?* Sheila had to make sure Lauren knew that she was in control and disobedience in her household would not be tolerated—not by Lauren or Lisa.

When Lauren came home from school, her mother was standing in the kitchen with the newspaper lying on the kitchen table. She walked into the kitchen talking about her day and how practice had gone. While listening to her daughter, Sheila walked over to the table and picked up the front page of the local news paper. All Lauren could do was stand there in shock, in horror, in humiliation. She had been caught red-handed. There was no way she could get herself out of this one. Lauren just stood there with nothing to say and wondered what her mother was getting ready to do. Her mother didn't whip them anymore; but at that moment Lauren wanted the whipping, so it would be over with quickly.

Her mother told her to sit down. "Why did you go behind my back and sign up for this trip, when I told you that you could not go in the first place?" Sheila was staring at her daughter with eyes as big as marbles. Lauren thought that at any moment her mom's eyes were going to pop out of their sockets. Lauren could not take the staring much longer. "I'm sorry, Ma. I am really sorry. I just thought if you saw how good the trip would be for me, that you would decide to let me go." Lauren didn't know what else to say to her mom and, for that matter, didn't have anything else to say. What she did was wrong and she knew it. Now she just wondered what was going to happen to her, since her mom found out about it from the newspaper.

"You disobeyed me, Lauren. I'm very disappointed in you. I know that this trip would be a great experience for you, but the way you went about it was wrong. And because you were disobedient, there will be consequences for your actions." Lauren knew that this was going to happen. Her mother did not play around when it came to lying and consequences. She had lied and got caught—she had no idea what her punishment would be. "I have decided to take your telephone away for a week. You can communicate with your friends in school, but not in your room on the phone. If you use the main house phone for personal reasons, I will take your phone for another week. Do you understand me?" Lauren nodded her head in disbelief because she knew she got off easy! "Yes ma'am."

Her mother wasn't finished talking, she had more to say. "Now, about this trip to Spain—yes, you can go. I think it will be a wonderful experience and opportunity for you." Lauren was ecstatic. Her mother was letting her go to Spain after all. "I'm proud of you for wanting to go to Spain. You're going to be exposed to another way of living, another culture and, more importantly, another language." Sheila was proud of her daughter and gave her a hug and kiss. "Just next time Lauren, please come to me so we can talk it out. I don't want to find out from other people about what's going on with my child."

"Yes, Ma'am," Lauren said as she gave her mother a hug and promised that she would never lie to her again. The thing Lauren hated the most was having her mom mad at her. *Boy, did I get out of this situation easy,* Lauren thought.

Chapter 6

Lauren Tells All

After they finished cleaning up her room and everything was back in place, Lauren realized that she would never be comfortable in that apartment again. They headed over to Jason's place for the night. It was dark by the time they left her apartment, which was comfortable for Lauren—if she wasn't visible to anyone, she wouldn't have to worry about ducking and dodging.

When they arrived at Jason's place, one of his roommates was still up playing a video game. Lauren said hello and walked quickly to his room. Jason stayed in the living room to chit chat with his roommate for a minute. Meanwhile, Lauren was in Jason's room looking around trying to find his gun. *I know his gun has got to be in here somewhere!* The investigators confiscated the gun he had at her apartment, when she was making comments about killing herself. They had no idea that he had two of them. *Ugh, I need to find his other gun before he comes in here. Where in the heck is that gun!*

Lauren wanted to commit suicide before Jason walked into the room. That way, she would not have to explain anything to him. *Of course, he will be sad, I hope; but I could leave this world knowing that he would never know the truth.* Her searching quickly came to an end when she heard Jason walking towards the room. *Dang it! I thought he was going to hang out there with his roommate much longer than that.*

Lauren decided that she would not be able to carry out her suicide that night. She would wait until the following morning, while Jason was at practice or in class. *This way, I'll have more time to look for his gun while he's away. By this time tomorrow night, I will be dead!* Lauren was anxious and ready to put an end to it all. She would carry out the ultimate defeat of a lifetime, something that would give her pride and joy—her prosecutors would not be able to prosecute her, because she would be dead! That feeling of satisfaction was what Lauren wanted. She refused to give the police investigators or prosecutors the opportunity to send her to prison.

Jason had a look of disgrace and disbelief on his face. He wanted answers and he wanted them now. He was tired of waiting. More importantly, he was upset that she had divulged information about her illegal activity to a bunch of complete strangers; but had little to say to him, her boyfriend. What Jason did not know was the fact that Lauren's failure to involve him in her little scheme is what kept him from having charges filed against him. Her lies are what kept him free and innocent.

Lauren knew the time had come for Jason to know what she had done—what was so horrible that had police investigators rambling through her apartment and had her retaining a criminal attorney. She wanted to lie so badly to him, because she knew that the truth would hurt; but as she stared into his eyes, she knew that she could not lie to him anymore. It was time to face the music, tell him everything and deal with the consequences as they come.

Lauren began by telling Jason about her family upbringing—how her parents had divorced when she was young. She told him that her mom couldn't buy her and her sister designer clothes like her classmates. She would buy their clothes from thrift stores and yard sales. They didn't dress like the other girls in school, because her mother didn't have the money. She said her low self-esteem began to develop early on when kids would pick on them for how they dressed. And she always thought that the other girls in her classes were much prettier than her.

Lauren never had a boyfriend, just friends. She recalled a time when she was in the sixth grade when she had die-hard crush on an eighth grade boy, who was very popular in school and played sports. She and her friend (along with some of their other classmates) had lunch with the seventh and eighth grade boys, so she would see him every day. After school she and a couple of friends would go to her house and make prank calls to some of the boys. The prank calls was something that she and her friends enjoyed doing, so she thought. A few weeks into the prank calls one of her friends decided to tell Lauren's secret crush what she had been doing after school. Lauren had no idea that her so-called friend had spoiled the surprise by telling her secret crush.

One day during lunch, Lauren's secret crush was waiting for her to sit down at the table. He walked over towards her and started calling her names and yelling at her about calling his house. He told Lauren, in front of everyone, that she was the ugliest four-eyed girl in the room and he would not be caught dead with her. Everyone at the table was laughing at Lauren, including her so-called friend. Lauren was embarrassed and mad at her friend, but there was nothing she could about it. She felt like a small ant that was being stepped on. That was the worst day of her life and she was only in the sixth grade.

After lunch Lauren went to the nurse's office and said that she was sick and needed to go home. Because her mother was working at the bakery and could not get off, she called her nana, Mama Pearl. Mama Pearl was her dad's mom, who lived nearby. Mama Pearl was furious with her son following the divorce and felt badly that her son did not own up to his responsibilities with her only grandkids. She knew that Sheila worked long hours at the bakery and always helped out anyway she could. *I wonder why Lauren is so* quiet. *This is not her usual behavior.* Mama Pearl knew something was wrong with Lauren.

When Mama Pearl asked Lauren what happened at school, Lauren started crying and told her nana everything. She felt so sorry for her granddaughter and decided to take her to McDonalds to cheer her up. When they left McDonalds Mama Pearl stopped by the bakery to let Sheila know she had picked up Lauren from school because she wasn't feeling well. "Your mom said that she will be by to pick you up when she gets off work."

When they pulled up to her nana's house, Lauren went straight to the bed to lie down. She wanted this day to hurry up and go away. She was embarrassed and, more importantly, she was mad at her so-called friend who stabbed her in the back. *How could she do that to me?* Mama Pearl entered the room later and sat quietly in her rocking chair. She could see that her granddaughter was hurt. As she sat there quietly rocking, looking out the bedroom window, they both heard the sounds of a school bus approaching. The high school kids were being dropped off at their stop. They could hear the laughter of the kids and conversations about what they would be doing later on.

But it was the conversation between a boy and a girl that caught Mama Pearl's attention. She motioned for Lauren to stand by the window and listen to the conversation that was taking place outside the window. They could hear a boy saying to a girl, "What time does your mom get off?" The girl told him that her mom was working late and would not get off until five or six that evening. The girl went on to tell the boy that he could stop by anytime and that she would be home waiting for him. When the girl walked off with her friends, Lauren and her nana could hear the boy telling his friends that something was going down when he got over to her house. "I'll call ya'll later on tonight to let you know how it went down."

While Lauren didn't know exactly what they were talking about, she did have a pretty good idea that it had nothing to do with homework. Her nana broke it down for her. "You see Lauren, that boy means that girl no good. He is going over to her house to have sex while her mom is still at work. Then, after he's done having sex with her, he's going to call up his buddies and tell them about it. The girl will probably want to keep it all a secret between the two of them, but it won't be. This is a small town and everyone will find out about her, and how easy she is."

Lauren was shocked at what her nana was telling her. *What would the guy gain from talking about his sexual activity with the girl?* "Lauren, these young boys out here are after one thing and one thing only. It's up to you to make sure that you don't allow yourself to be placed in a position where these boys or any other boy will be able to talk about you and say that they have had you sexually, you hear?"

Lauren nodded her head and thought that boy was mean for running his mouth; but, at the same time, shame on that girl for wanting to have sex with him. Didn't she know that he was going to talk about her? Oh, there was just so much to learn and know about boys. Lauren's nana went on to tell her that making prank phone calls was wrong and that my friends and I had no business doing such a thing. She told Lauren that when you do something bad to someone else, bad will come back on you. Unfortunately, the bad came back on Lauren during lunch and she was humiliated by her secret crush in front of everyone! Then her nana said something that did not make any sense to Lauren at the time. She said, "Obedience is better than sacrifice, Baby."

Jason knew that Lauren had issues with low self-esteem. He would always try and tell her how pretty she was, because she was. She was different than a lot of the girls he had dealt with in the past, which is why he liked her. She was all about her books and education and would always talk about wanting to travel overseas to different countries. And she had the most beautiful smile that could light up an entire room. She was tiny and cute and he enjoyed spending time with her. It was something about her small town personality and behavior that he admired and loved, that made her so innocent when it came to living in the city life, Yeah, he cheated her on with other girls, he was in college and he was an athlete and that's just what the guys did. But, behind the scenes, she was the only one for him. She was kind and sweet and had just the perfect personality for him. She didn't care about his basketball status or any of that—all she really cared about was spending quality time with him.

As Jason continued listening to Lauren, he could not help but notice the tears swelling up in her eyes and how they fell down her cheeks. His girlfriend was in trouble, he just didn't know how much trouble. He wanted to put his arms around her and hold her real tight—something he would always do to make her feel safe and secure. But he couldn't hold her right now; he needed to know what was going on that required her to retain an attorney.

Sitting on Jason's bed, she told him everything. She knew that he was probably upset and their relationship would be over, but she didn't care. She was getting it all out. She would be committing suicide in the morning anyway, so his opinions and thoughts about her didn't matter at this point. *This will be all over in the morning.* She continued on, telling him how it all started.

She moved to Orlando following graduation from high school after learning that a few of her classmates were going there. Contrary to what everyone in her north Florida town thought, she had nothing in place for furthering her education after graduation. She had no idea as to what she would be doing or where she would be going. She had not applied at any colleges.

Continuing on, Lauren told Jason that she was currently under investigation by the United States Postal Service for Possession of Stolen Mail and Credit Card Fraud! According to the postal inspectors, the investigation had been underway for nearly a year and they had gathered enough evidence against her to file charges. "That is why I had to meet with an attorney," she told Jason. He sat there looking at Lauren in complete disbelief. He stared at Lauren, as if she was a ghost! His girlfriend was being investigated for participation in an illegal criminal act. He could not believe the words that were coming out of her mouth.

Lauren continued on with her explanation by telling Jason how it started. When she moved into her apartment complex following graduation from high school, her mother told her that she would be responsible for her own bills. So, with that conversation in the back of her mind, Lauren immediately found work at a customer service call center. She took classes in the morning and went to work in the afternoons. She had been working at her job for nearly two years when she met Jason; that is when her life changed.

Jason was an only child from Houston, Texas. His parents were killed in a car accident when he was ten, so he was raised by his aunt and uncle. He was attending the university on a basketball scholarship. When Lauren and Jason first met, she had no plans on falling in love with him and she knew his feelings were mutual. She enjoyed his company and the time they spent with each other. They enjoyed bowling and going to the movies. She would lend her car to him, for him to go places like basketball practice, study hall, or even just hang to out with his home boys. She enjoyed making him happy and keeping a smile on his face. Lauren, on the other hand, was totally opposite. She had a few friends, but hanging out wasn't her thing. She would prefer to spend her nights cuddled up with Jason watching a movie or buying him gifts.

She admired how he would always come back to her place after hanging out all night with his friends. It made her feel loved, wanted, secure and protected when he came back to her. She never quite understood why she felt that way, but she did. She wanted to be loved and hugged, because it made her feel close to him. What really attracted her to him in their relationship was the simple fact that he never tried to be intimate with her. At first she thought he was gay; but later learned that he respected her as a person, as a female, and wanted to get to know her for who she was. While he did want to be with her in that way, he knew that she was too special to mistreat and felt that he would wait until the time was right.

Lauren thought about the first time Jason came over to her apartment. He was dressed in a nice Tommy Hilfiger polo shirt with his 'pop' collar. He had on a pair of Tommy slacks and pair of open toe sandals for men. She had never seen a guy wear sandals before; but she had to admit, he looked good. She noticed immediately that he dressed a lot different than what she was used to seeing guys wear. His hair was a nice low fade that complimented his face and his gorgeous light brown eyes. He was and still is a very handsome young man—words that Lauren would continue to tell him for years to come.

She wasn't expecting him to be dressed so nicely and was somewhat embarrassed with what she was wearing. She had on a pair of grey sweatpants and old shirt from high school. It was a little cool in her apartment, so she had on a pair of socks to keep her feet warm. Her hair was tied up in a ponytail with front bangs. Her mother always told her that she and her sister had large foreheads and they should wear bangs to keep it covered—so her bangs were for comfort and security and to keep him from looking at her forehead.

Jason sat there and continued listening to Lauren talk about her insecurity. He knew she had some self-esteem issues but didn't think it was that bad. In the back of his mind he always thought she had a little jealousy in her, but never imagined it to be this out of control. He thought about the time when his ex girlfriend, Gina, found out about Lauren. Gina was livid when she found out that Jason had moved on and made it her business to let Lauren know who she was.

One Monday morning before her class started, Lauren was talking to a few girls in her math class. They would hang out occasionally and would talk casually about what they did over the weekend. Lauren told the girls that she had met this guy named Jason who played basketball at the school. When she was describing how Jason looked, when one of the girls said they thought they knew him. Lauren didn't pay any attention to what the girl said and kept talking about her new friend, Jason. When class was over the girls said their goodbyes and parted ways until their next class.

The following Wednesday, Lauren got ready for her math class as usual, When she arrived on campus she spotted one of the girls from her class, They chatted a little out in the parking lot and then walked towards the building where their math class was being held, As they approached the building, they saw another student standing outside with the other girls from the class, Lauren had no idea who the girl was and thought she was a new student that enrolled in the class late, Then, out of nowhere, the girl stepped up to Lauren and started questioning her about Jason, Turns out, the girl was Jason's ex, Gina.

Gina was getting loud and was pointing her finger as she walked towards Lauren, Needless to say, Lauren was surprised. She had no idea that Jason was dating another girl. Apparently, he met Gina a year or so ago, before Lauren moved there. And, according to Gina, she and Jason were still a couple. Lauren had no idea if she was getting ready to fight Gina or not. *I have never gotten in a fight before in my life. But I know one thing, Jason and I are finished!*

She didn't want to have anything to do with Gina or Jason. Their relationship was over. The one thing she was thankful for was the fact that she did not have sex with him. She would be one female he could not talk about. *I am so glad I overheard those boys when I was at my nana's house.* Lauren was so grateful that her nana had that conversation with her. It was a conversation she would never forget.

Later that night, Jason called her wanting to talk. It seemed as though Gina was so upset after finding out that Jason had moved on, that she called him repeatedly and left several messages on his answering machine. He really liked Lauren and didn't want anything more to do with Gina. He saved the messages for Lauren to hear as proof that they were not together. So, Lauren went over to Jason's dorm room and they talked. She told him what happened earlier that day before class with Gina and that she didn't want to be involved in any mess between him and his ex. Jason reassured her that he and Gina were history and that he had moved on. Moments into their conversation Jason's phone rang again. It was Gina. Jason didn't pick up the phone so she called again and again. All in all, Gina called his phone continuously until Jason took the phone off the hook. Lauren didn't know who to believe.

She had never been involved in any type of relationship drama so she was a little concerned. She already was dealing with low self-esteem issues and she didn't have time for any more drama. She was a little skeptical about her relationship with Jason; but she was interested in him, in spite of Gina. Lauren knew that if her relationship with Jason didn't work out, she would probably never find another guy like him. So, she did what she thought was right, she forgave him and decided she would take a chance with their relationship. The following morning, Lauren went to campus to speak with an admissions counselor about the incident with Gina. The counselor withdrew Lauren from the class and put her into another math class on a different day and time.

Shortly after the incident between her and Gina, Lauren received notice from her job at the call center that they were downsizing and reorganizing and they would be eliminating positions. Because she didn't get any help from her mother to pay her rent, she immediately started looking for employment elsewhere. She gained a lot of experience working in the call center and felt confident that she would find another job. She knew she was responsible for her own bills and her mother constantly reminded her of that whenever she would call home asking for money. There were many times she wished that she didn't have to work. A lot of the people she had met in college were full time students and didn't work. She wanted desperately to be like them. She just wanted to go to school and not have to worry about bills. She didn't want to drop out of school and go back home. So she had to find another job.

Chapter 7

Lauren Works in the Mailroom

One afternoon before work, Lauren stopped by her mailbox to see if she had any mail. She noticed a flyer on the mailbox kiosk. It said that the apartment complex was hiring college students to work part time in the complex and, if you were a resident there, your rent would be free. As Lauren read the flyer through, she thought how awesome it would be to have free rent. With her worries of paying rent taken care of, she could find a part time job that would pay for her cell phone bill and other miscellaneous items. Lauren walked hurriedly back to her car and drove straight to the leasing office. This would be one day she would be late to the call center!

When Lauren walked into the leasing office, she noticed another student sitting there answering the phones—this would be a simple cake walk for free rent. She told the student that she was there to speak with someone about the flyer that was posted on the mailbox kiosk. The student nodded, got up, and went into another office. A few moments later she returned with a Spanish man following her. He asked if she lived in the complex. "Yes, Sir," she replied. Lauren followed him back to his office, where they sat down to talk about the job opportunity. His name was Elliot and he was the office manager. He had filled all the office positions, but he still had two openings left in the mailroom. The work days were Monday, Wednesday, and Friday from noon until six in the evening, which included free rent. Elliot told her there would be days when she would have to work beyond six in the evening, but the job was fairly easy. Once the mail was sorted and delivered to the mailboxes, the student workers would return back to the leasing office and do homework—someone had to be at the mailroom in case residents came to pick up larger packages that couldn't be placed in the mailbox.

Lauren sat there listening to Elliot, but all she could think about was the free rent— and that she would not have to drive to work. Yes! Finally, something good was happening for her. When the conversation was over, Elliot offered the job to Lauren and said she could start in two weeks. She would only have to pay her rent one more time before the free part kicked in. Lauren was excited! When she arrived at her call center job, she immediately informed her supervisor that she would be resigning in two weeks!

That night when Jason came over to see her, she told him about her new job at the apartment complex. He was happy for her and suggested they go out to celebrate. He took her out to a nice Italian restaurant that had just opened up a few months ago. It was Lauren's first time at an Italian restaurant and she was nervous. She had to impress Jason at dinner—it was her way to show him that she cared about him. They had never been to this restaurant before so Lauren didn't know what was on the menu. She insisted that they go someplace else, but Jason wanted to try out the new Italian place. *I hate going places where I am not familiar with their food.* Growing up as a child Lauren's mom didn't take her and her sister to eat out at restaurants, so she was a little nervous whenever someone suggested eating out, especially with Jason. She knew how to behave and conduct herself whenever she did eat out in public, but the awkward feeling of looking through a menu, not knowing what the food items are, is what Lauren didn't like.

Lauren had been at her new job in the apartment complex as the mail clerk for about six weeks. She was attending school full time and had even found a part time job working for a local security company, where she was able to earn some extra cash. Her relationship with Jason was going great and she was feeling pretty good about herself. She wanted to do something special for him and decided to go to the mall and buy him an outfit. She picked out a nice pair of jeans with a nice designer shirt, had it gift wrapped, and bought a card to go with it. When he came over that night, she surprised him with the gift. He was overjoyed, but asked her why she had done it. She told him that she wanted to let him know how much he meant to her and that she appreciated him. Lauren knew that he didn't work and didn't quite have the funds to buy things, so she took it upon herself to do it. Besides, she enjoyed being in a position to do it for him. She didn't have a problem with buying him clothes or giving him money. He was her man and she knew that if she bought things for him, he would not want to leave her.

As the weeks went by, Lauren continued to buy Jason gifts. There were times when they would go out to dinner and a movie and he would motion to pay, but she would override him and pull out the money. He didn't refuse and she didn't mind. More importantly, they were together and she wanted to be around him. It was during the times when he wasn't around her, when he wanted to hang out with his friends and go to the club, that she felt most vulnerable and unloved or that he was cheating on her. While she never had proof, Lauren knew that Jason was cheating on her, which affected her low self-esteem.

Because he hung out with his friends and went to the club, she knew she had to work harder to prove to him that she was his one and only—even if that meant she had to buy him more things. And so she did. She continued to give him more and more clothes, jewelry, and money. She would buy him greeting cards for no reason, just to show him how much she wanted to be with him. And the more she bought, the more he smiled—and she felt loved and protected and safe.

Then one day it finally happened. They were in her apartment having a conversation and he mentioned to her that he was thinking about buying some shoes. But they were not just any old kind of shoes; they were the new Michael Jordan shoes. Lauren knew she had to go and buy them for him, but she didn't have any money. She had maxed out the only two credit cards that she owned. She had to figure out a way to buy her boyfriend the new pair of Jordans before someone else did. But how could she accomplish it? She had no other means of money. Her job in the mailroom was compensated in the form of free rent and she didn't get paid from her security job for another week. She had to think quickly and move fast, because she had to buy those shoes for her man. He wanted them and it was her responsibility to get them.

Lauren felt useless and hopeless as Jason's girlfriend since she didn't have the money to buy the shoes. She thought to herself that if Jason was with one of the other girls from campus, they would buy him those Jordans the moment he asked for them. *Why couldn't I come from a wealthy family with money!* Lauren knew she had to find a way to buy those shoes for her boyfriend before someone else did. She didn't know how but she knew she had to find a way—and she had better do it fast.

Chapter 8

Lauren's Criminal Activity Begins

Lauren was in the mailroom, sitting in her station and sorting the mail. Her job was to separate the incoming mail by buildings. Once all the mail had been separated by building numbers, the staff would then sort the mail for each building by apartment numbers. After all the mail was placed into the mail slots, they would rubber band it together and place it in mail bins for delivery. The apartment complex was made up of three different phases. Each phase contained a mail kiosk and the staff was responsible for their own kiosk.

Lauren was sorting the mail when she came across an envelope with a hard textured feel on the outside. *I wonder what's inside this envelope. It feels like a credit card or something.* The letter was addressed to a student living in the complex who, in Lauren's mind, wouldn't even notice if it was delivered or not. She thought about the time when she received an envelope very similar to the one she was holding. Inside the envelope was the credit card she had been waiting on, Lauren just knew there was a credit card inside the envelope she was holding. So she wouldn't draw attention to herself, she took the envelope and placed it into one of the mail bins that was in her phase. She continued sorting the mail and noticed several other letters that she believed also contained credit cards in them. She placed them in the same mail bin as the first one.

When they were done sorting the mail for all phases, Lauren went back to a table and pulled out a magazine to read, She tried to take her mind off the envelopes, but she couldn't, It kept going back to the envelopes and how the texture of them felt like credit cards, She knew if that if she could get her hands on one of those credit cards, she could buy her man the shoes he wanted before someone else did, She didn't know how she came up with the idea to steal the mail, but it would be perfect if they were credit cards, She had to figure out how to get those letters inside her apartment without being caught, She later realized that it wasn't as hard as it might seem.

Lauren knew that taking the credit cards was probably wrong, but she had to do something to get those shoes for her boyfriend. *I've got to get him those shoes, and I will.* The one and only thing on her mind was getting those shoes. When it was time to deliver the mail to the kiosks, she decided not to go through with it and removed the envelopes from the mail bins—she didn't have the nerve built up to carry it out.

Over the next couple of days all Lauren did was think about buying those shoes for Jason, She didn't have any money—she was broke, When she got to the mailroom there were only two of them scheduled to work that day, One of the student workers left early due to illness, so it was left up to either Lauren or the other student worker to deliver the mail to the kiosks, They finished sorting the mail and decided that Lauren would deliver it to all three phases, while the other student worker maintained the mailroom, She had come up with a plan to get the credit cards inside her apartment, Instead of placing the mail into the correct mailbox, Lauren decided to place them in her mailbox.

Lauren was excited about her new adventure. She decided that when she found one of those envelopes she would pull it out of the stack and set it aside. So no one would get suspicious, she would place the envelopes into her own mailbox and retrieve her mail later that night when she got in from work. The plan seemed like a great idea at the time and it worked. *If it was not for me to get the mail, then I wouldn't have been the one to do the mail run in the first place.* But she did do the mail run that day, which meant it was meant to be.

There were some residents standing near the mail kiosk waiting on Lauren to finish, and they had no idea what Lauren was doing. She was a little nervous at the idea of using a credit card that didn't belong to her, but the more she thought about it the more she realized that no one would be getting hurt. She had never done anything like this before, and she had to admit, she was a little nervous. *Well, if someone had a problem with their credit card all they have to do is call the company and report the card lost or stolen. No big deal.* She just wanted to buy her man his shoes.

About an hour or so after she had delivered all the mail, Lauren returned back to the mailroom. She had about four hours left to go before the mailroom closed and she was nervous. She went back and forth about having placed someone else's mail in her mailbox. *I know what I am doing is not right, but I have to get money to buy Jason his shoes. I'll do it this one time and then I'll stop.* Lauren tried to behave as normally as possible. Her other coworker was still in the mailroom with her and she didn't want to look suspicious.

When Lauren got off work, she quickly walked back to her apartment building, took a shower, changed into something more comfortable, and then walked over to her mailbox kiosk. She unlocked the door with her key and removed all the contents, including the extra pieces of mail that didn't belong to her. She closed the box and walked back to her apartment. There were two pieces of mail for her roommate and the rest were for her. Anxious and excited, she went back to her bedroom and closed the door. She was on a mission and could not be bothered. She ripped open the envelopes and to her surprise every envelope had a credit card inside. She was excited and nervous at the same time—she had found a way to keep her man happy without damaging her pockets.

Lauren knew from her own two credit cards that a social security number and zip code was needed to activate them. She figured the same would be true for the ones she now had in her room. There were five credit cards in her hand that didn't belong to her. One would prove to be a real challenge, because it was a man's name. So Lauren decided it would be easier to use the cards with female names. The next thing was to find out what the balances were on the cards. In order to do that she had to call the number on the back of the card. She was surprised when the first card she tried didn't need verification. It was a replacement card for a department store in the mall that sold men's clothing. More importantly, it had a credit limit of $1500 that she could use on whatever merchandise she wanted.

Lauren was so excited she could hardly contain herself. There was no way she would tell anyone about her new found fortune; but she knew it was what she needed to get what she wanted, which would make her man happy and love her! Lauren knew what she was doing was not right, but she justified her actions by telling herself that she deserved to be happy and that no one would get hurt. It was just a piece of plastic with a credit limit that would allow her to buy her boyfriend nice gifts whenever she wanted. Besides, she had worked hard and was tired of struggling and not having anything tangible to show for it. It was time for her to enjoy life and have some fun! No one would have to know. It was a little secret that she would keep to herself. How could she possibly get in trouble, if she didn't tell anyone what she was doing? Right?

The following morning Lauren got up early to put her plan into action. It was a Saturday and she didn't have to work in the mailroom. She was also off from her part time security job. The night before she had thought long and hard on how she would go to the mall, pick out a few items to purchase on the stolen credit card. Before she would pay for the items, she would throw the cashier off by asking if she could make a payment on the card first. She had no room for error so her plan had to work. The one drawback that she had anticipated was that the name on the credit card did not match her name on her driver's license. She decided that if her plan did not work the way she had thought, she would simply walk away from it all.

When she pulled into the mall parking lot she didn't anticipate any worries. She was a young college student at the mall doing some shopping for her boyfriend. She had one thing in mind and on her shopping list and that was to buy those shoes. She rarely went to the mall; and if she did, it was only to buy something for Jason. She got out of her car and walked in with her credit card in her wallet. She was browsing through all the clothes in the store and found herself in the women's department.

There were so many nice clothes she contemplated buying with the credit card, but she couldn't. She got the card for one reason and that was to buy those shoes for Jason. But the clothes were pretty and for a moment she imagined herself being dressed up like the girls she saw on the university campus and in her apartment complex. She knew that her clothes were a lot different than what the other college girls were wearing, but she didn't have the money to buy them. She thought to herself that if she did have clothes like these, how much more attractive and pretty she would be to Jason. She didn't have a strategy as to how many items she would pick out to buy. All she knew was that the credit card she had in her wallet had a credit limit of $1500 and she had to buy something to see if her plan would work.

Lauren slowly picked out three shirts and three pairs of jeans and went into the dressing room. She tried the items on, loved how they fit, and decided they would be her first items. She quickly got dressed and walked out of the dressing room with her clothes in hand. She didn't even bother to look at the price tags, because really it didn't matter—it wasn't her money anyway. Lauren walked up to the register. There was one other person in front of her, but no one else. The sales associate was a young girl, maybe a high school student working there part time. When the sales associate was finished with the customer it was Lauren's turn. *It's now or never,* she said to herself,

In spite of what she was doing, Lauren was a good person with a bubbly personality. She used her personality to play to the sales associate's weakness. Lauren immediately started talking to her and asked if the store was hiring and how long she had been there. The conversation was friendly and on point until the sales associate asked to see some identification. Lauren knew she didn't have any identification to support the credit card, but she somehow remained calm, cool, and collected—she did not want to break under pressure. She slowly opened up her purse and pulled out her wallet. *Oh my goodness, she is watching me. I have to think fast or I won't be able to use the credit card.* Then she remembered having some money inside her wallet. She had to come up with something quick because the sales associate was waiting.

"Hey, before you charge these items to my card, I need to pay on my bill. I don't want to have one of those late fees assessed," Lauren said while handing the associate fifty dollars. The sales associate nodded and took the payment. She then told Lauren that she was doing a good thing by making her payment before the deadline. Lauren continued to engage in conversation and started talking about her boyfriend, that his birthday was coming up and she had no idea what to buy him. The sales associate started laughing and said that she too had the same problem with her boyfriend. *Wow, this was much easier than I thought.* Lauren was telling the associate how she wanted to buy her boyfriend a pair of Jordans, but they didn't sell them in that store. So the associate suggested to Lauren that she buy her boyfriend a gift card to make it easier for him to pick out his own gift.

The gift cards were at the register and could be purchased from any register in the store. When her items were finalized the associate asked if she wanted to include a gift card with her purchases. Lauren agreed and bought a gift card for Jason in the amount of two hundred dollars. When the associate was finished ringing up the items, she swiped the card through the machine and it went through. When the associate was finished, she put all the items in the gift bag, including the gift card, and wrapped them up. Lauren signed off on the credit card receipt, thanked the associate and walked out. The sales transaction was complete and she had not been stopped by security. Wow! It was so simple to go in and buy something with the credit card. Lauren was in heaven on cloud nine!

Before she left the register the sales associate reminded her about the open job opportunities in the store and gave her an employment application to fill out. Lauren thanked her and headed out the door. As she walked pass the trash can, she tossed the application into it. She didn't need a job—she was the mail clerk at her apartment complex with access to credit cards that gave her all the financial freedom she could want! *My life is great!*

When Lauren got back in her car she was happy, nervous, and emotional all at once. She completed the impossible mission without even breaking a sweat. She was so thrilled and proud of herself, but a little disappointed that she wasn't able to buy Jason the shoes he wanted. She hoped the two hundred dollar gift card would make up for it. She considered returning to the store to buy another gift card, but decided against it. *I'll wait to do it for another special occasion,* she thought to herself.

Jason wasn't home that Saturday morning. His basketball team had traveled out of state for a game and was not scheduled to return until later that night. He normally would call her after he got back to his dorm and she would go and pick him up. Because he was gone on Saturdays for games, they would always spend Sundays together. He was going to be so surprised when she gave him his gift. She could hardly wait! And she was right. When Jason got back in town from his basketball game, Lauren went and picked him up. She had not seen him for almost two whole days and was excited to have him back. She knew that he could have been anywhere that night, but he chose to come over to her apartment and chill out with her.

When they got back to her apartment, she told him she had a gift for him. She gave him the greeting card first that read, *I missed you.* When he opened the card up, there was a gift card for two hundred dollars inside, all for him. His face lit up when he saw the amount on the gift card. He thanked her and then asked her why she bought it for him. She quickly told him that she understood he wasn't working and that she knew he needed money to buy clothes and shoes. She knew that with the gift card he could buy what he needed. She said that since she didn't know his taste or style in clothes, she thought he would like a gift card more. As strange as it may have sounded, Jason didn't think twice about her actions. He just figured she probably came from a wealthy family and loved to buy him things.

The following morning when they woke up, Lauren suggested they go to the mall so he could use his gift card. They decided to grab lunch while at the mall. When they arrived at the mall and walked into the department store, Lauren could see the happiness on Jason's face—that made her feel good. She had finally met someone who really liked her and she enjoyed making him happy and putting a smile on his face. He picked out a few items, paid for them with the gift card, and then they left. They walked around the mall and went into a few department stores. She watched him as he looked at different items in the stores. He tried on shoes, hats, and looked at jewelry. She knew she had to do whatever it took to get these items for him. He never asked her to buy him anything, but that didn't matter. He didn't have to ask her. Lauren felt that it was her responsibility to make him happy. She knew that as long as she could keep him happy, he would always want to be with her—and that was more important than anything.

Chapter 9

LAUREN USES MORE CREDIT CARDS

It had been six months since Lauren first used someone else's credit card. Her life was headed in a positive direction and her relationship with Jason was better than she could ask for. There were still minor issues involving his ex-girlfriend, Gina, but it was nothing that a couple of items from the mall couldn't resolve. Her job at the mailroom was going fine. She had even perfected her game of taking the credit cards—by intercepting the delinquent letters from creditors and destroying them in the trash. The credit card holders didn't need to know what was going on. She continued to put other resident's mail in her mailbox and would retrieve them after work. She was on a roll and enjoying every minute of it. When she maxed out one credit card, she started using another one. It was almost like an addiction with credit cards. Being able to buy Jason whatever he wanted gave her a rush. *Maybe that's how drug addicts feel when they are high.* But Lauren wasn't a drug addict. In fact, no one could have possibly imagined Lauren stealing credit cards. It was her little secret and she vowed to keep it that way.

Lauren started stashing the maxed out credit cards in a duffel bag inside her closet. Often times she thought about cutting them up and tossing them in the trash, but that was time consuming. No one else used her closet, and she was the last person anyone would suspect of using credit cards that didn't belong to her.

She wasn't worried about getting caught because, in her mind, she was innocent and no one was getting hurt in the process. Besides, her one and only mission was to please her boyfriend. She never viewed her actions as wrong and she never once thought about how others could potentially be hurt. Since she didn't think about her actions, she wasn't too concerned with the consequences either. She would constantly tell herself that she wasn't a bad person, After all, she wasn't using drugs or killing anyone; she was just using credit cards that were in someone else's name.

So Lauren continued this behavior in the mailroom—before she knew it, a year had passed. Credit cards were coming into the mailroom left and right and she was taking them. Some had MasterCard logos and others had Visa logos. She was so good that she even got the pin numbers to go with the credit cards, which would let her withdraw money. She needed the cash more than anything, because she enjoyed giving Jason money to spend on whatever he wanted. She loved taking care of her man. She really didn't buy things for herself. She would get her hair done and a pedicure every other weekend, but nothing more. There were times she would buy an outfit or two for herself, but not much else. She liked the way she looked and, more importantly, her boyfriend was still happy. They didn't take vacations, but they would spend time at local theme parks and eating at different restaurants. She loved every minute of it.

In the beginning, when she first started taking the credit cards, she would only carry it with her when she needed to buy Jason something. Then she would put it back in her secret hiding spot. But now, Lauren carried as many as five credit cards on her at any time. She had the pin numbers written down on the back of them—in case she needed to stop and get some money. She ate out a lot and rarely cooked. She ended up quitting her part time security job a few months after she started stealing the credit cards. She was part time working the third shift and didn't like being at work when she could be with Jason. And besides, she felt she was making a good earning with the stolen credit cards. She later found a part time job at wireless retail outlet store, where she worked four hours a day in the evening. She decided that if she maintained a steady part time job and continued with her studies on a full time basis, no one would suspect her of anything. There was no stopping Lauren—she was to the point where she had everything (so she thought) and saw her life completely perfect.

A year into her credit card scheme, some of the residents started coming into the mailroom complaining about missing mail from family and friends. Lauren knew that she had to keep the residents from going into the leasing office, so she decided to stop stealing the mail for awhile. It did place her in a difficult position because Christmas was around the corner and she depended on the credit cards to get by. She had around twenty five hundred dollars stashed away in her room for when Jason was a little low or needed something at the last minute. Her number one priority was to make sure her man was taken care—he could not go without.

After laying low for about a month, her money stash started to dry up. She had to get back on her game plan and start stealing more cards. The Christmas holiday was fast approaching and she had to make sure Jason had gifts. Hundreds of Christmas cards were flooding the mailroom every single day. *I know there has got to be money inside some of these Christmas cards.* And Lauren was right—there was as much as two hundred dollars in some of the cards. She started taking the Christmas cards and putting them into her mailbox. When she would get home and open up the cards, she was amazed to see the many different gift cards that family members were sending in the mail. She didn't realize that people actually sent cash in a card, but they did. One time she opened up a card that had five hundred dollars in cash and five hundred dollars in food and shopping gift cards. There were some Christmas cards with checks that were made payable to residents, but Lauren didn't touch those. She knew it would be big trouble if she tried to cash a check in someone else's name. *I'll stick to my credit cards and opening up Christmas cards.* She tore up all the checks and put them in the garbage. She had no reason for keeping them around when she couldn't use them.

Lauren got so caught up in stealing the credit cards and Christmas cards that she started ignoring the resident's complaints. She became obsessed with her plan. She had literally become addicted to the money and being able to buy things for Jason. She wanted it to be like Christmas for him on a daily basis. And as long as she worked in the mailroom, he would have Christmas twenty-four seven.

At the start of the fall semester the university began mailing out parking decals to all the students. The parking decals were mandatory and were required in order to park on campus. The mailroom received tons and tons of parking decals for students. One day while in the mailroom, Lauren decided to take a few of the decals to see if Jason had any friends that needed one. Parking decals were expensive, so she thought she would help them out. A month or so after Lauren started taking the decals they were notified by the leasing office that complaints were starting to come in about missing parking decals. The leasing office thought that the mailroom was being lazy and not putting the decals in the correct box—but that wasn't it at all. It was Lauren that was behind the parking decal issue. Since she couldn't really benefit from the parking decals, she decided to stop taking them—to her, the credit cards were a better return on her investment.

As the months rolled by, Lauren and Jason's relationship was still going strong. She stopped going home on weekends to see her sister and mother. She was not about to give up any opportunity to work in the mailroom and steal credit cards. Jason would fly back home when basketball was not in season. Sometimes Lauren would accompany him and sometimes she wouldn't. She enjoyed spending every single minute with him. She missed going back home to visit her mom, sister, and nana but she just didn't have the time. Besides, whenever her mom wasn't working in the bakery, she would be too busy putting down someone else's child. *If she only knew what her daughter was into, I bet she would stop talking about people then.* She was pretty sure that it would be more than just her mom who would be upset and disappointed if they ever found out what she was doing. But they wouldn't; in fact, Lauren vowed to take her little secret to the grave.

Lauren was approaching her junior year at the university. She had taken the majority of her classes at the local community college and was excited about being a step closer to graduating. Ironic as it may seem, she applied and was accepted into the criminal justice program. She figured that she knew firsthand what to look for in criminals. *Maybe I can even go to law school.* She often thought about going to law school, but never applied. She thought about continuing on with the mailroom after graduation—*I wouldn't have to worry about rent.* Lauren had become quite comfortable in the mailroom. She had it all planned out in her mind, so she thought. She would later find out that her ending was just about to begin.

When she started taking classes at the university, she was exposed to more people. She realized she had to step her game up with how she dressed in comparison to the other girls on campus. Money wasn't an issue, she had plenty of it. What she didn't know was how to coordinate her clothes. So she would watch Jason, who dressed flawlessly—how he wore his clothes. He had plenty of style to rock. She started paying attention to the way people dressed in magazines and on television. When she went to the mall, she would buy the outfit that was on the mannequin. But no matter how many clothes she bought or how she wore her hair, she never felt pretty enough. What she failed to realize was that her looks had nothing to do with Jason—it was her with all the issues. Jason always told her she was pretty, but deep down inside she believed she was ugly. In fact, she always thought she was ugly.

Chapter 10

LAUREN'S WARNING
BEFORE DESTRUCTION

It had been nearly two years since Lauren used her first credit card. She managed to keep it a secret this entire time, but she was starting to get bored. No one had suspected her to be the one behind all the stealing, so she thought.

Lauren carried a green mini notebook, in which she kept her active cards. She took that green notebook with her everywhere she went. Jason never paid any attention to it because he thought it was something that she used for her classes. One day she was on campus for class, but she was sitting on a bench waiting for Jason to get out of his class. Her class didn't start for another hour, so she wanted to see if Jason wanted to grab a bite to eat. When she spotted Jason walking up towards her, she got up to greet him with a kiss and they walked off. Seconds after they left the area, Lauren realized she left her green notebook on the bench. *Oh no! My credit cards are in there.* She told Jason about her notebook and went back to get it, but when she got there it was gone. Just like that, the credit cards that she used so faithfully were gone.

There were a couple of students hanging around the area so she asked if any of them seen her notebook, but they hadn't. At that point, Lauren became upset—someone had taken her notebook and she didn't know who. Not only were the stolen credit cards inside her notebook, but her class schedule and several other documents were in there that could easily link her to the stolen credit cards. *How could I be so stupid!* Lauren didn't know what to do. She couldn't say anything to Jason because he had no idea she was even stealing credit cards. She walked around the building to see if she could spot her green notebook, but it was nowhere in sight. Her notebook was gone. Her heart began to race and flutter at the same time. Her knees were shaking and she was out of breath. She felt as if she was dying away. She thought she was going to have an asthma attack. She could not believe how careless she was with her notebook. She prayed so desperately that whoever found it would just trash it. She wanted to tell Jason about the credit cards, but knew that if he found out he would probably leave her. So she had to act as if didn't matter—it was only a notebook.

When she walked back outside to Jason, she wanted to cry; but she had to control herself. *It may not be anything. Maybe who ever took my notebook never looked inside and just threw it away.* At least that is what she hoped, but deep down inside something was telling her that she had messed up big time. Jason asked her if she found the notebook, but she had not. He could tell by her behavior that she was upset because she didn't speak much for the rest of the afternoon. He figured she must have left some money inside her notebook and now it was gone. *No big deal, she has plenty of money. I am sure she will hit up the ATM and withdraw more.*

Jason sat there listening in awe as Lauren told him everything. He was starting to put the pieces of the puzzle together. He could not believe that Lauren, his very own girlfriend, was involved in a serious credit card scheme. He was outraged at her for even doing such a horrible thing. He continued to listen, as she described the events that led up to her arrest.

After she had lost the notebook, she decided to lay low for a while and not touch any more credit cards. She also took some time off from the mailroom. She wanted to see if anything would come of the stolen notebook; but because she was young and thought she was above the law, she wasn't that concerned.

A week into her time off Lauren realized that her money stash was starting to get low. She needed to get back into the mailroom so she could build up her reserve—Jason might need something so she had to get back on her job. So Lauren returned to the mailroom and continued with her activity of stealing credit cards and pin numbers. Deep down inside she really wanted to stop stealing the credit cards, but her love for the money and her boyfriend's happiness just wouldn't allow it. Besides, she had become dependent on them as her means of survival. If it was not meant for her to be doing this, she would have stopped a long time ago. So she continued on and on, stealing more and more credit cards, something she had learned to do so well.

Lauren realized she had to replace the cards that were in her green notebook. The first thing she did was buy a new billfold wallet. She started carrying a smaller wallet and did away with notebooks. Since she lost the green one, she wouldn't take any more chances. She returned back to work so she could get more credit cards. A few months passed and no one ever approached her about the notebook. She kept waiting to see if she would receive a letter or something, but nothing ever happened. She eventually stopped worrying about her missing notebook and moved on with her life.

She continued to use the credit cards to take her boyfriend out and buy him nice things. He was so clueless about the entire situation. She enjoyed every minute of it and was delighted in his happiness. She never really cared about her own happiness or if she even was happy at all. She just kept reminding herself that what she was doing was not in vain—it was all for Jason.

It had almost been a year since she lost the notebook on campus and she was feeling like she was on top of the world! Her classes were moving along and she was finally in her senior year of college. She had no complaints.

A new restaurant opened up in the area and both she and Jason were eager to go try it out. In the short few years they had been together, she became comfortable with eating out at different restaurants. Jason had taken the time to show her how to eat certain foods when in public. He told her that companies would sometimes interview potential applicants in restaurants to see if they could eat properly. She was very thankful that he was teaching her and showing her things that no one else did. Her fear of eating in public restaurants had been cured, thanks to him.

When they arrived at the restaurant there was a twenty minute wait—everyone wanted to try out this new place. When she and Jason finally were seated, they were ready to order. After placing their order they sat there and talked about their day and how class went. She was telling Jason that she didn't do well on one of her midterm exams and how disappointed she was since she had done a lot of studying. As usual, he reminded her how smart and pretty she was and that he was sure she would do well in the class. Moments later a server brought out their food. After they were done eating Jason suggested they go to the movies. They paid for their food and left. Lauren was so busy talking to Jason that she left her purse on the seat.

It was while they were at the movies Lauren realized she had left her purse at the new restaurant. She had done it again! *Oh my goodness! How could I be so darn stupid to leave my purse!* She was furious. Inside her purse was her wallet that had the credit cards in it, along with her driver's license. How could she do this again! She had to go back to the restaurant and get her purse or she could have some serious problems. She insisted that they leave the movies, which they did. They left the movies and headed back to the restaurant. At this point, Lauren was in deep panic mode, because her ID was the one sure thing in her purse that would definitely link her to those credit cards. How could she be so stupid and dumb?

When they arrived at the restaurant, it was closed. Lauren got out of the car and ran to the front door, but they had already locked up for the evening. She pressed her face against the window and saw people cleaning up. She started knocking on the window until she got the attention of one of the workers. The worker motioned to her that the restaurant was closed, but Lauren didn't care. She continued to knock and bang on the window until another person, possibly the manager, appeared to the front door entrance.

"Can I help you?" the lady said. Lauren explained that she had dined there earlier that evening and may have left her purse in one of the booths. The lady slowly looked at Lauren and asked her to describe the purse and any belongings that were in it. So Lauren began to describe her purse to the lady. While Lauren was describing it, she noticed the facial expression of the lady, as if something wasn't right. The lady then asked Lauren to follow her inside so she could bring her the purse.

As Lauren waited inside the restaurant she begin to have a sick feeling, as if something terrible was about to happen. She stood there for about five minutes and wondered what was taking the lady so long. She looked around the restaurant and saw a group of people hovered in a small office. She could hear voices, but couldn't make out what they were saying. Then she saw a shadow of a light, blinking on and off, like a copy machine or a camera. She didn't know what was going on, but was getting more nervous by the minute. Finally, the lady came back out with her purse and a smirk on her face. Lauren kindly thanked her and hurried out of the restaurant.

When she got back in the car Jason asked her why it took so long. She told him that they were looking through her purse to insure that the identification and contents matched—and that routine paperwork had to be completed when items are left in their store, per company policy. But as they drove off and back to her apartment, Lauren knew deep down that something was not right. The behavior of that manager and the little smirk on her face were red flags that something horrible was about to happen.

Chapter 11

LAUREN HAS A TALK WITH THE POLICE

The following morning Lauren was getting ready to go to work at the mailroom. She was still thinking about the manager's behavior from the night before. She remembered hearing something that sounded like a copier machine or scanner, but wasn't quite sure. She was still getting ready when she heard a knock. She wasn't expecting company and Jason was already on campus—she had no clue as to who it might be. She walked over to the door and looked out the peephole—a police officer was standing there! *Oh no! I knew it. I knew it. Those people at that restaurant called the police on me! I can't go to jail. What am I going to do?* Lauren didn't know what to do. She was sure she had been caught!

When Lauren opened the door, he identified himself as Officer Williams with the Orange County Police Department. He asked Lauren if he could step inside her apartment for a moment. She opened the door wider and motioned for Officer Williams to come inside. She had no idea what was going to happen to her. There were all kinds of things running through her head. He told her that a report was made last night about possible credit card fraud and that her driver's license was found in the wallet. He was there to conduct a follow up on the report.

Lauren thought back to the night before, when she was at the restaurant waiting to get her purse back. That noise she heard and the blinking lights that she saw was a copy machine. They were making copies of the items in her wallet for documentation to show the police. How could they do that to her? She was furious! If only they had minded their own business, she wouldn't be in this predicament. And now, here at her apartment in broad daylight, a police officer was talking to her. *I will never eat there again.*

He asked her to follow him outside and back to his car. Lauren just knew she was going to jail that day—but not yet. Lauren put her book bag down and followed the officer downstairs to his car. He told her to have a seat in the back. Up until this point she had never been inside of a police car. *I know I am going to jail.* While she was sitting in the back seat of the car, he was standing outside of the car, talking on the phone. She couldn't really hear what was being said but she knew that he was on the phone with someone important. *Why did I let myself get into this mess? I am done stealing credit cards!* Then all of sudden, just like that, he was opening the back door to let her out and told her she was free to go. He asked her if she wanted a copy of the report and she told him no. *There is no way I wanted to have anything to remind me of this day.* She literally ran back upstairs to her apartment as fast as she could. She had to finish getting ready for work. She had to be to the mailroom to start work at noon and it was already 11:30.

Chapter 12

LAUREN'S MAILROOM OFFICE MEETING

When Lauren arrived at the mailroom, she behaved as if everything was normal. There were three of them on the schedule to work and she was the second to arrive. The other employee showed up ten minutes later. After about an hour or so, one of the leasing officers came to the mailroom to let the staff know of a mandatory meeting to be held immediately following work. Lauren didn't think twice about the meeting and thought it was about time they were being included.

She decided while sorting the mail that she wouldn't steal any credit cards that day. Having the police officer show up at her front door earlier that morning had her spooked. She didn't want to touch anything that didn't have her name on it. She thought she would wait for it to blow over, like the parking decal incident and her lost notebook. She thought about telling Jason about the police incident from that morning, but decided not to. He didn't know about anything else so far and figured it was better if he didn't know.

Since the meeting didn't start until seven, she decided to go home for a few minutes to settle down—she had had a rough morning. When she got to the meeting everyone was standing around talking and drinking punch. She wasn't in the mood to socialize and felt so out of place. *I wish this meeting would hurry up already.* Everyone was standing around, eager to hear what the mandatory meeting was all about. Well, it turns out that the mailroom was getting a new makeover and updated shelves. There would be some minor construction going on and contractors coming in and out of the mailroom. The office manager, Elliot, wanted everyone to be aware of what was going on, since it would be happening during normal business hours. He said that work would begin as early the next day. *They called a mandatory meeting for this!* Lauren was ready to go home. After talking about the mailroom makeover, Elliot went over some other changes that would be occurring in the complex regarding students and parking. None of the rest applied to Lauren; she wasn't even paying attention. The meeting lasted thirty minutes too long and she was ready to go see Jason.

When the meeting was over, Lauren walked hurriedly back to her apartment. Jason was coming over that night and she wanted to go to the store and buy him an *I Love You* card. Part of her daily routine was giving him cards, and she had run low on them.

As the days passed, Lauren kept working in the mailroom. She soon forgot about the incident with the police officer and her purse being left at that restaurant. She vowed never to eat there again, because of the betrayal she felt from the employees. She knew that it would be a smart thing for her to stop stealing credit cards and putting them into her mailbox, but she didn't. In fact, she was so addicted that she had to steal a piece of mail every day she worked. She had become addicted to making her boyfriend happy—to her, nothing else mattered.

She had been working at the mailroom for nearly two and half years and was finally approaching her last two semesters. She was a senior, getting ready to graduate from college. Despite losing her notebook on campus and stealing the parking decals and credit cards, she still felt pretty good about herself. She told herself over and over that she is a good person with a good heart and no one had gotten hurt from stolen credit cards. She made it this far without being caught and figured it someone else's loss and her gain. *I am sure that if I wasn't stealing the credit cards, somebody else would.* The mailroom was her source of income; even with all the complaints flooding in from residents, she wasn't going to stop—not just yet. She did think about quitting a couple of times, but she just couldn't. She had become comfortable where she was and she wasn't going anywhere. She was graduating from college pretty soon and wanted to keep getting all the free rent she possibly could.

The construction workers started working in the mailroom. They were putting in new shelves, making cosmetic changes to enhance its features. Lauren didn't think they were doing much of anything, except wasting time and getting in her way. She rarely paid them any attention and kept stealing credit cards. She got so bold with the mail that she started taking it directly from the mailroom. She didn't even bother putting it into her mailbox anymore. *Going back out at night to check my mailbox is just too much.* It was much easier for her to steal the mail directly from mailroom—only this time, it would be her last.

Chapter 13

LAUREN IS APPROACHED BY THE POSTAL INSPECTORS

Roughly a week or so after the construction workers started working in the mailroom, Lauren was approached by the United States Postal Inspectors—she finally got caught. She was being investigated for credit card and mail fraud.

It was a normal morning. She woke up and the first thing she did was check the balances on the credit cards. This was a standard routine of hers, something she did just about every other day—it had become second nature. She went through her little money stash to find only six hundred dollars remaining. Knowing that the weekend was coming, she had to go and stock up, just in case Jason wanted something. Taking care of him was always her primary goal—that would never change for her. She took pleasure in taking care of him.

She finished getting dressed and decided to run by an ATM machine to get some money. When she pulled out of the parking lot, there was an old blue Cherokee jeep and silver Crown Victoria that pulled out behind her. She didn't think anything about it, so she kept driving. As she was exiting the complex, she decided she would go to the ATM machine on campus since it was much closer for her. She was at the light waiting to turn into the university when she looked in her rearview mirror—the same two cars were about two cars behind her. She didn't think much about the two cars, but decided she would drive around the campus to see if they were following her. To her surprise, everywhere she drove the two cars were right behind her. *Are they following me?* She started to get a funny feeling inside, because she was sure they were following her—there was no mistake about it.

She decided to drive up to campus security to let them know of her suspicions. When she pulled up, she told the security officer on duty that she was on campus for class and suspected she was being followed by the two cars in her rearview mirror. She gave a description of the vehicles to the security officer and he said he would look into it. After giving the report, she drove off. She saw the security officer stop the blue jeep first and figured they would get to the bottom of it. She knew the two cars following her had nothing to do with her stealing the credit cards—it was something she had kept from everyone, including God. She figured it was probably Gina, the ex. *That's what she deserves for trying to follow me. That girl needs to get a life and get over Jason already.* Lauren would find out later that the campus security were already aware of the postal inspectors.

She finally drove over near the ATM machine to get some money. She found a parking spot next to a thirty minute parking meter. She was so focused on getting money out of the ATM that she didn't even realize the blue Jeep and the silver Crown Victoria had parked directly behind her. She got out of her car, walked through one of the buildings, and went through a side corridor that led up to the ATM. She withdrew some money from a few cards, grabbed the receipts, and walked back to her car. She was back in her car, sitting at the light when she looked in her rearview mirror again—the same two cars were behind her again at the light. She knew it was nobody, but Gina. *How does this girl know where I live?* She and Jason would be having a little talk when he came over that night. She took her cell phone out in case she needed to call the police—she had no time for drama in her life. She didn't have class that morning and she wanted to get back to her bed, so she could lie down before working in the mailroom.

The moment Lauren pulled in the front of her apartment building she heard police sirens behind her. When she looked up in her rearview mirror, the same two cars had pulled in behind her. It was the police—she had been caught. Only this time, it was for real.

All Lauren could think about was jail—she was going to jail. As she was opening up her car door to get out, she was approached by a lady, Postal Inspector Jasmine Lipzoni. She identified who she was and then gave Lauren two options. They could either go downtown to their office and talk or they could go upstairs to her apartment. Of course, Lauren didn't want to go to their office and said they could go upstairs to her apartment. All she wanted them to do was turn off the sirens and flashing lights—it was way too much attention. Besides, she felt more comfortable in her place. There were two more postal inspectors with her— Michael Stonecole and Denyse Nodi. Inspector Lipzoni seemed to be more in control and domineering from day one. Before they walked up to Lauren's apartment, Inspector Lipzoni asked if she could search her and her vehicle. Lauren said, "Yes." Lauren knew that she had money and credit cards on her since she had just came from the ATM. She also knew she was in some serious trouble. Inspector Stonecole was searching her car, while she was being patted down by Inspector Nodi. Lipzoni was just standing there, watching everything like she had just caught the biggest drug dealer in town. She was looking at Lauren with disgust and hatefulness. Lauren could sense her dislike for her from the very beginning.

When Inspector Nodi pulled out the cash from her pocket, she asked Lauren if it was money from her personal credit card. She told Inspector Nodi that none of it was hers, hoping that they could hurry up to her apartment. Residents were starting to come out and see what was going on with all the flashing police lights. But Inspector Lipzoni seemed to be enjoying every minute of it. It was almost as if she was holding Lauren downstairs on purpose.

Finally, Lauren asked if they could please go upstairs and she would tell them everything. Inspectors Nodi and Lipzoni came upstairs with Lauren, while Inspector Stonecole kept searching her vehicle—he came up to her apartment later.

After they were inside the lead inspector, Lipzoni, told Lauren that she was being investigated for ongoing theft in the mailroom at her apartment complex. They knew that it was a large scheme and that she was not working alone. They wanted names of everyone involved—who else was in on the theft. Lauren told them flat out that she was not working with anyone else, that she had done everything by herself. Inspector Lipzoni did not believe her; she just knew Lauren was lying. But Lauren was telling them the truth—there was no one else involved. She had done all the stealing alone.

Moments later Inspector Stonecole entered the apartment. He informed Lizponi that he had searched inside of Lauren's vehicle and didn't find anything. Lipzoni then asked Lauren if they could search her apartment. Lauren said, "Yes." She thought that if she was nice to the inspectors and provided them with everything they wanted, they would not press charges against her. So while Stonecole and Lipzoni went through Lauren's one bedroom apartment, she was sitting at the table with Nodi, telling her everything. Lauren told the inspector when it all started and why she did it. She told her that she wanted to stop, but she couldn't.

While Lauren was at the table with Nodi, she heard the male inspector say he was going down to get mail bins—he returned a few minutes later with about five to six mail bins. Lauren had no idea what was going on in her room. She could not see inside her bedroom from where she was sitting. Finally, when Nodi was done questioning Lauren, they walked to her bedroom. Lauren's room was a complete disaster. Her clothes had been taken off the rack and dumped everywhere. Her mattress was pulled aside and was leaning against the wall. But what made Lauren sick to her stomach more than anything was seeing her duffel bag—they found her secret hiding place with all the credit cards she had used and kept over the years. *Why didn't I get rid of them?* Lauren knew that her life was over. The mail bins that were brought in were filled to the top with all kinds of papers. Lauren knew that they would use those papers against her as evidence.

All Lauren could do was just stand there while the inspectors went through her room. All the evidence and proof that they would need was right there. The one thing she most feared had finally happened—she got caught. She was scared and nervous and knew she was going to be in big trouble. Inspector Lipzoni kept telling her that she should be ashamed of herself for doing what she did. She told Lauren that people like her deserved to be in prison and that she would burn in hell for everything she had done—and that is when Lauren started crying hysterically. Lipzoni told her she would probably serve some serious prison time for her crime and that she would forever be labeled as a convicted felon, the lowest criminal on the earth.

Lauren kept crying—she knew she wasn't a bad person. Sure, she was stealing credit cards, but that didn't make her a bad person. She had a wonderful personality and was outgoing and well liked, she wasn't a criminal. They kept going through her room and talking to her at the same time. Inspector Stonecole looked into her nightstand and pulled out the gun, which was registered to her boyfriend, Jason. He handed the gun over to the lead inspector, Lipzoni, who called it in to see if it was legal. It was. She always made sure that Jason was legitimate—there was nothing illegal about him.

They told her that they suspected Jason was involved, but it turned out he was clean. Apparently, the inspectors met with Jason a few days earlier while he was at practice. Lauren knew that he would be questioning her big time when he got over there. *He probably is not going to want anything to do with me now.* Her life had spiraled out of control in a matter of seconds. The more she thought about prison, the more she cried. The thought of going to prison just didn't sit well, mentally.

Lauren couldn't take it anymore and started telling the inspectors that she would kill herself before going to prison. The thought of serving time and being away from Jason was just too much for her. Inspector Nodi started talking to her as if they were friends. She began to tell her that everything would be alright as long as she did what they asked. But Lauren wasn't paying her any attention, her mind was on prison. She started shaking and hyperventilating, something she did whenever she became nervous. Her mother had always told her that if she made her bed hard, she would have to lie in it. She just didn't think she would have to lie in prison for what she did. Concerned with talk of suicide, Inspector Lipzoni told Lauren they were keeping the gun for safety reasons and Jason would have to contact them to get it back. She then asked Lauren if there were any more weapons inside her apartment. Lauren told her no.

All three of them continued to search Lauren's apartment as she sat there quietly, looking on. Her crying had slowed down a little, but she was still sobbing. Then finally, they were packing up to leave. Lauren asked the lead inspector, Lipzoni, if anybody would find out what she had done. Lipzoni told her that people would find out only if she did not cooperate. She told Lauren she would be in touch with her and they walked out of her apartment, leaving her room just the way it was.

As the three of them exited the apartment Lipzoni turned to Lauren and said, "Don't bother going to the mailroom, your leasing office has already been notified of your actions." That is when Lauren realized where she had seen them before—they were the construction workers in the mailroom. Inspector Nodi left her jacket inside the apartment and had to run back in to get it. As she was walking out of the apartment she turned to Lauren and quietly said, "DeJohnson. Brendan DeJohnson is an attorney. Retain him."

Chapter 14

LAUREN'S SUICIDE ATTEMPT

Jason continued listening to Lauren. He could hardly believe what he was hearing. There was no way his girlfriend was capable of doing something like this. He knew she had issues with low self-esteem, but he just didn't think it was that bad. *How could someone as pretty as her have low self-esteem.* Lauren was gorgeous and beautiful and he would tell her that often—not because he wanted to, but because it was the truth.

By the time Lauren finished telling Jason about her credit card scheme, she was exhausted. Her eyes were so red and swollen from crying, it looked like someone had beaten her beyond recognition. As they sat on the bed, complete silence engulfed his room. It was so quiet they could hear each other's heart beat. The seconds turned into minutes, which felt like an eternity. Lauren didn't know what else to say or do and Jason was speechless beyond his wildest dreams.

How could he have known that the gifts from his girlfriend could jeopardize her future, and his future as well—and what about him? How could she have placed him in a position that might cost him his college education, career, and life? He had never been in this kind of predicament before and really didn't know what more he could say or do to ease Lauren's pain. He was feeling hurt himself. When he asked her why she had done it, she just looked at him and shrugged her shoulders. She couldn't even explain her behavior or any of her actions. One thing just led to another, and to another, and then this. Neither one of them knew that her low self-esteem played such a major role in her decisions.

The following morning Jason got ready for practice. He told Lauren that he would be back to check on her when he got the chance. Before he walked out the door, he gave her a hug and told her that everything would be okay.

Soon after Jason left, Lauren laid back down for a few minutes. Her mind started racing back and forth about what she had done over the past two years. She tried to come up with reasons as to why she did it, but she couldn't. The longer she laid there, the more upset she became about getting caught. *If only I had been more careful.* She was still in denial by thinking she hadn't done anything wrong—it was everyone else's fault.

None of it mattered anyway, because she was going to kill herself. She had nothing else to live for and she was not going to prison. She realized she would have to do it quickly—Jason would be coming back from practice in a few hours to check on her. She got up and started looking through his dressers for his other gun. She knew he kept it in his room somewhere; she just had to find it. His room was very small, so her places to look were limited. After searching for about thirty minutes, the only thing she found was a black chess box that had a combination lock on it. Since she couldn't get her hands on the gun, Lauren sat back down on the bed to rethink how to end her life. She would overdose on prescription drugs—but Jason didn't have any prescriptions in his room and there was no way she was leaving his dorm room in broad daylight.

The hours were passing by and Lauren started to think about going to prison. She had seen horrible things on television that happened to women in prison and she did not want anything to happen to her. As she thought about going to prison, she started to cry again. *Am I really that bad of a person?* All she did was use credit cards that didn't belong to her—she didn't kill anyone. She didn't know what to do. If only she hadn't used those credit cards, she wouldn't be in this predicament. *But if I hadn't lost that stupid notebook or left my purse in that restaurant, I wouldn't even be in this mess.* Should have, would have, and could have didn't matter at this point. What mattered was that she got caught and she would have to pay the price for her actions, even if it meant prison time.

When Jason returned from practice, Lauren was in bed asleep. It was around noon and practice was over for the day. He woke Lauren up and asked her if she had eaten anything. With all that had been going on, Lauren hadn't even thought about eating. She had food in her apartment, but she dared not to go back there. She didn't even know if she was still on the lease or not. What she did know is that she had to hurry up and find somewhere else to stay before they evicted her from her apartment following the investigation. She was pretty sure with all the information the inspectors had on her, her free rent would be over! The lead postal inspector, Lipzoni, had told her not to bother going into work, which led Lauren to believe that her job in the mailroom was over as well. She told Jason that she had to go look for another apartment because she wasn't going back there—she didn't even want to sleep there. She just wanted to go, get all her clothes, put them in her car, and never set foot in her old apartment again.

Jason reminded her that she would have to leave the dorm, if she was going to go look for a place to stay. He assured her that no one knew about the investigation and that the paranoia of everyone looking at her was all in her imagination. But Lauren didn't believe him at all. In fact, she felt that if the investigators could follow her, then anyone could be following her. After about an hour of convincing her, Lauren finally gathered up the courage to leave; but she made sure to put one of Jason's baseball caps on before they walked out of his dorm room.

Because she wouldn't go back to her apartment and she didn't want to go back to north Florida, Lauren found an apartment that day that was just a few miles from the university. She was still within driving distance to attend classes and then could hop on the expressway to go to her part time evening job. She was so thankful that she had kept her second job while working in the mailroom. Later that night, they went back to her apartment to pack her things. She didn't have to worry about moving the bed or dresser as those items were furnished with the apartment. In less than an hour, her things were packed in large garbage bags that were placed in her car. Jason was exhausted and had to get up early the next morning for practice. He had not planned on helping Lauren move that night, but he did. Her new apartment was on the first floor, so they wouldn't have far to carry her bags.

Chapter 15

LAUREN TRIED TO MOVE ON WITH HER LIFE

Nearly four months passed since the morning Lauren was questioned by the postal inspectors. She had no idea what was going on with her case and didn't really care to know. She decided to continue on with her life as if it was no big deal and everything was normal. She was in her final semester at the university and was excited about graduating from college. She didn't have any plans in mind, so she decided to take advantage of internship opportunities that were being offered. She was still working part time jobs here and there to pay her rent. She really missed the free rent from her old apartment but, given the circumstances, it was something she had to get over.

Brendan DeJohnson was supposed to be one of the best attorneys in town. He was recommended by one of the postal inspectors, Nodi, who whispered his name. His retainer fee was $15,000 and his office agreed she could make monthly payments—she had to have the best representation. He had a stellar reputation and was known for keeping some of the worst criminals from going to prison. Lauren thought that if her attorney could get big time drug kingpins off, then her case would be a cake walk. She didn't keep in touch with him like she should have. In the beginning she would call his office weekly to see what was going on and if there was anything she needed to do. He would always tell her to stay out of trouble, keep a job, and keep her address updated—nothing else. She slowly stopped calling his office because she didn't think it was that serious. No arrest had been made so she began telling herself that everything would go away. She knew he would do everything in his power to keep her from going to prison.

She eventually told her mother about the investigation. Her mother was very surprise when Lauren told her the bad news. She told Lauren to move back home, but Lauren refused. Besides, she didn't think she would go to prison. She told her mother that they were going to give her probation for a few years and everything would be fine. She felt that the less her mother and sister knew the better.

Her relationship with Jason was still going strong. He didn't leave her after she told him what was going on, but he wasn't as faithful either. They would still go out and do things together in the daytime, but at night he would hang out with his friends and hook up with other girls. Lauren would always call him on his lies and how she suspected him of cheating on her, but she had no real proof. His ex girlfriend, Gina, was still in the picture, even though Jason would not admit it. But Lauren knew her man, and she knew he was a liar. But she felt as though she deserved every bit of it, the cheating and all. She had been unfaithful in their relationship, also—stealing credit cards and using money that didn't belong to her. But in spite of the cheating, she loved Jason whole heartedly and only wanted to be with him.

Jason's patience was starting to wear thin with Lauren. She was in a whole lot of trouble and he didn't feel the need to be caught up in her mess. He was a young college student with a promising basketball career ahead of him—he had hopes of playing in the NBA. He did care for Lauren a lot, but he just didn't know about taking a chance with her. He had to wait and see how all the allegations and charges will play out. He felt betrayed, deceived, and cheated by her; but at the same time he didn't want to leave her, because he felt sorry for her.

Lauren wanted to do more for Jason but financially, she couldn't. She had no money and all her credit cards were gone. There was no way she could take care of him on a part time salary. Lauren tried to move on with her life, but she couldn't escape the thoughts of suicide. She wanted so desperately to end her life and avoid going through the embarrassment and shame of what she had done— and going to prison. Whenever she was alone in her apartment, she would try to think of ways to commit suicide and actually carry it out. She would have done it back in Jason's room but couldn't find his other gun. She knew that one single gunshot to the head would guarantee her death.

One night after she and Jason got into an argument about him cheating, she took a bottle of Tylenol. She knew he was going out to meet some girl and was just tired of everything—she had nothing else to live for. She wanted to end all of the sadness and disappointment she felt with herself. She stared at herself in the mirror and called herself all kinds of ugly names. *Look at how stupid you are. You are so ugly. You can't even keep a man. No one will ever want you when they find out what you did. You would be better off dead.*

Lauren believed everything that came out of her mouth. She believed she was ugly and that she would always be at the bottom. She started crying as she reached for the bottle of Tylenol in her cabinet. She kneeled down on the floor with the bottle in her hands. *It's either now or never.* Lauren twisted open the top, threw her head back, and swallowed all the Tylenol. She stood back up and grabbed a bottle of Motrin, sat back down on the floor, and swallowed all of them. She tried standing up, but her knees were feeling weak. She knew Jason had a bottle of liquor underneath her kitchen cabinet. She fell down as she walked toward the kitchen, then crawled the rest of the way—her vision was blurred. She made her way to Jason's liquor, opened the bottle, and took about two gulps.

Jason was on his way to the club. He could not be around Lauren that night. Every day she was accusing him of something and now it was cheating. Sure, he talked to other girls, but it wasn't anything serious. He had to find some way to occupy his time and to deal with all the mess. He did feel bad about how he had stormed out her apartment. She was crying hysterically, begging him not to go out. *She just doesn't understand. Why did she have to go and do what she did?* He felt really bad for her and wished that he could make it all better—but he couldn't. When he got to the club he realized that he had left his wallet on the dresser. *Man, I have to drive all the way back to the apartment for my wallet.* He hopped back into his car and drove back to the apartment. When he pulled up to the apartment he could see that Lauren still had on all the lights. He walked into the apartment, bracing himself for another argument. He walked past the living room and bathroom to get to their bedroom—no Lauren. She would have normally been standing at the front door the minute he walked in. He grabbed his wallet and walked out—still no Lauren. He walked around to go into the kitchen when he saw her—lying on the kitchen floor, vomit everywhere.

He immediately ran over to her and started calling her name out, but no answer. He took his cell phone out and called 911. Within minutes, the paramedics rushed her to the hospital due to a drug overdose. When they arrived at the hospital, Lauren was unresponsive. They rushed her immediately into surgery to try and save her—and they did. Doctors told Jason that if he hadn't returned to the apartment when he did, Lauren would have been dead. Her first attempt at suicide was unsuccessful.

Following her overdose incident, Lauren wasn't focused on her studies and decided to withdraw from her classes to pull herself together. She was a little disappointed that her suicide attempt did not go as planned, but was thankful to have Jason around for awhile. But a month or so later, he started going back out to the club and hanging out late with his friends. Lauren became depressed again and started having suicidal thoughts. Instead of carrying out the actual suicide, she started having manic depression symptoms.

She withdrew from all her friends and stopped going places in the daytime. When she did leave her apartment, it was only at night. She thought everyone was following her and would drive an extra twenty or thirty minutes out of her way, just to make sure. She and Jason would argue more and more and each argument became worse. Her self esteem issues were not getting any better either. She looked at herself in the mirror and called herself ugly and stupid, because of the mess she was in. She didn't feel as pretty as the other girls that she saw in passing or on campus. The only thing she cared about was Jason and how she had hurt him with her lies. She wanted to fix everything and make it right, but it was too late. She thought of herself as a low life and someone who would never amount to anything. She oftentimes would think about her actions and justify them, by saying that no one was hurt or killed—but she was wrong. What she had done was against the law and illegal.

She remembered her mother telling her as a little girl *that if you make your bed hard you must lie in it*. Now Lauren believed she understood what her mother meant by those words. She would have to lie in her hard bed for her actions—she just never thought her hard bed would be in prison.

Chapter 16

LAUREN'S SNAKE DREAM

Facing the reality of graduating from college in a few months, she decided it was time to look for a fulltime job. She searched the classified ads and came across a financial aid position with a local independent college. After two interviews she was offered the position and was scheduled to start in a week. She was excited and couldn't wait to tell Jason about her job offer. He had gone home for the summer, but was scheduled to return the day before she started her new job.

It had been a few weeks since she had last seen him. The time away did them both some good. It allowed Lauren to get out of the apartment and find a new job. As for Jason, he had an opportunity to hang out with his family back home and forgot about the mess that Lauren was in. He decided to fly back in town a day earlier so he could spend time with her. Once practice started, he knew that his schedule would be very hectic.

When he arrived at the apartment she was bubbling with excitement. She was happy to see him and excited to tell him about her new job. She gave him a big hug and a kiss. They decided to go out and grab something to eat. She told him all about her interview and how it was such an easy job. She was looking forward to possibly starting a career there. He saw the happiness in her eyes and was glad that she was doing better. The next day they decided to just hang around the apartment and rest since they both would have a busy Monday.

During the middle of the night, Lauren woke up in a sweat; she had a bad dream. She tried to go back to sleep, but she couldn't. She was tossing and turning. Each time she went back to sleep, she continued to have the same dream—a dream about snakes. There were so many of them in her dream that she was crying in her sleep because the dream felt so real to her. She eventually went off to sleep only to have the alarm clock go off two hours later. Jason had basketball practice and Lauren had to go to work. It would be her first and last day on the job.

While getting dressed, she told Jason about her snake dream. In her dream she was surrounded by pythons and rattle snakes. There were thousands and thousands of them and there was no way she could escape. Each time she woke up and went back to sleep, she would dream about the snakes again. Jason told her that snakes represent the enemy and that she should plead the blood of Jesus over her life. Lauren had no idea what Jason was talking about and just figured it was the food he ate the night before.

They finished getting dressed and Jason left the apartment first, telling her that he would see her later on that day. Thirty minutes later, Lauren left for work. She was so happy that she had found this new job. *It's time that I move on with my life and look forward to my future.* Despite her stealing the credit cards and getting into all that trouble, she was feeling upbeat. Life was starting to look good for her. She arrived at the parking lot, her heart beating rapidly from the excitement of starting her new job. She wore a pair of black dress pants with a sleeveless gold blouse and black open toe sandals. She had a black sweater with her, in case the office was a little cool.

When she walked into the building, she was greeted by a receptionist. Lauren identified herself as a new employee working in the Office of Financial Aid. The receptionist was really nice and asked Lauren to have a seat while she contacted them. A few seconds later Tina, the Financial Aid Manager, arrived and greeted

Lauren. Tina and Lauren walked down the hall and entered another office—there were several other employees there to whom she was introduced. Tina informed Lauren that she would be shadowing Naomi for one to two weeks or until she became comfortable with the computer system and her job duties.

Lauren and Naomi had been working for nearly three hours when in walked a middle aged lady. Lauren and the lady's eyes locked for a few seconds and then Lauren went back to listening to Naomi. The lady stopped and asked to see the manager and the employee pointed to Tina's office. The lady walked over to Tina's office, while looking back at Lauren. Lauren started to get nervous because she knew that lady looked familiar. When the unknown lady walked into Tina's office, Lauren was unable to concentrate—she was too busy watching the lady and Tina in the office. As the coworker kept talking Lauren pretended to listen, but she couldn't. She was trying to figure out how or why she felt as though she knew that lady.

Lauren was still watching the lady, when all of sudden she remembered her from her apartment—it was the postal inspector! Inspector Lipzoni had came to her job, but why? As soon as Lauren realized who the lady was and what was going on, Lipzoni and her boss walked out of the office and towards Lauren. Lipzoni took out a pair of handcuffs and asked Lauren to stand up—she then started reading Lauren her Miranda rights. Lauren was horrified! She was being arrested on charges of credit card and mail fraud— it had finally happened! And of all places, it was happening on her new job, in front of everyone.

Lauren stood up and placed her hands behind her back. She was going to jail. A federal judge had signed off on an indictment, which gave them the right to arrest her. But how? How did they know where she was? Lipzoni proceeded to handcuff Lauren right in the financial aid office where everyone could see. There were students in the office talking with other financial aid counselors; her manager was standing there alongside her; her coworker was staring at her in disbelief. There were no words that could possibly describe the emotions and feelings that Lauren was experiencing. She wanted to cry and scream. She was so embarrassed!

As Lipzoni escorted Lauren out of the building, Lauren passed the receptionist who had greeted her earlier with a smile and pleasant attitude; but now she didn't seem so pleasant, she looked puzzled and confused. Lauren wanted so badly to run out of there, but she couldn't. And to make things worse, Lipzoni was making it a point to walk her out as slowly as possible. A few feet passed the receptionist desk, Lipzoni stopped to make a call on her cell phone. "Yeah, we got her; she's in handcuffs now." People were walking past Lauren as she stood in the hallway, handcuffed. She could not believe what was happening. Students were coming out of the classroom looking, staring, and making gestures toward Lauren. All she could do was just stand there—she was so humiliated. Lauren felt that Lipzoni was making this big scene on purpose.

When they finally walked outside, she put Lauren in the back seat of an unmarked police car and asked if she wanted to make a phone call. Lauren decided that her one and only phone call would be to her lawyer—then he could contact her family.

Chapter 17

LAUREN IS ARRESTED

As Lauren sat in the back of the police car, all she could do was cry. The day she dreaded had finally come—she was going to prison. They were taking her to the Orange County Jail off of 33rd Street. The drive took forever and she cried the entire time. As they pulled up to the jail, Lauren could see three or four news reporters standing outside the entrance. When the investigator opened the door to get her out, the reporters were filming the entire scene. Lauren realized then that it would be on the news. She knew that the media would make a huge deal about it, turning it into a media circus——and that is exactly what happened.

Once she got through the media frenzy, Lauren was processed, finger printed, and booked into the Orange County Jail. She was in a holding cell for a few hours before they moved her to another area. That area had a phone booth inside, where the inmates were able to make local calls for free. Lauren called Jason. The first time she tried she didn't get an answer, so she left him a message telling him where she was. Jason was at practice, so it took Lauren two more times before he finally picked up.

She was then moved to another cell that was much bigger than the previous one. The ladies in the cell all looked rough, like they belonged in there. Lauren was scared but she dared not show any emotions or tears in front of the other inmates. There was a phone inside the holding cell which she used to call Jason. She learned through Jason how they found her—not that she was hiding from them or anyone. Apparently an hour after Jason got to practice the postal inspectors came to the university and asked him if they knew where she was working. Jason told them about her new job. He said that he didn't realize they were coming there to arrest her or he would not have told them anything. Nevertheless, she was now in jail and the time had come for Lauren to face the consequences.

After being in the second holding area for awhile, they called the female inmates out and told them they would be showering and getting ready for bed. Lauren thought that it was probably starting to get dark outside, but she didn't have any way to tell the time. There were no windows to look out of, there was nothing. The rooms were very old with gang writings on the walls. The inside of the cells kind of reminded her of how old abandoned buildings looked like after they had been run down and written on.

She was allowed to make one more phone call before they exited the holding area. She called Jason again to let him know that she was moving out the cell and would be in touch with him when she could. On the way to the showers, Lauren decided that she wasn't going to get undressed in front of the other inmates and refused to shower. A female correctional officer looked at Lauren and told her that she might want to reconsider because it would be awhile before she would be released from the county jail. After hearing that information, Lauren was really scared and nervous, but she still refused the shower.

Once all the inmates were done showering, they were escorted into another room with bunk beds and mattresses on the floor. Lauren found a floor mattress near the end of the room in the corner and decided that would be her sleeping area. Seconds later the lights went out and Lauren could hear ongoing chattering by the inmates. She could hear some of the inmates telling people to be quiet and go to sleep. But Lauren just laid there on the mattress.

It was so thin she could feel the hardness of the cemented floors. The entire place smelled of dirty urine and feces. It was pitch black dark in the cell except for a few hall lights. The room was cold and dark, eerie and shallow. It was cold inside the room and she wanted a blanket, but there was none. Her orange jumpsuit was really big on her, so she used it to keep warm by putting her hands inside of it.

Alone and angry with herself, she lay on the mattress and thought about the last few months. How dark would her future be, now that she was headed to prison? She had messed up big time and now she was going to pay the price. She prayed it was all a dream and she would wake up, like she did that morning dreaming about the snakes.

The snakes! She had dreamed about the snakes and Jason told her that it represented the enemy and she had to plead the blood of Jesus, but she had not. In fact, she considered this entire investigation a big joke until now. She was in serious trouble with the law and she knew it. It was time for her to pay her debt to society for the crime that she had committed, the very crime she had failed to own up to.

She wanted to wake up from this horrible nightmare and have her life back. But, in fact, this was anything but a nightmare—it was reality. Lauren had some real consequences to face for her actions! In fact, this was only the beginning of the reality that would follow, with a healthy price she had to pay. She thought about the one time she carried out her suicide attempt. *I wouldn't be here in this jail if Jason had of not came back to the apartment. I was supposed to be dead by now, not sitting in jail. Now everyone is going to know what I did.* Lauren lay there quietly crying until she fell asleep.

Chapter 18

LAUREN'S FIRST COURT APPEARANCE

The following morning Lauren was awakened by a correctional officer. She followed the officer to a small room where she was handed a bag which contained her clothes. After she got dressed, she was led to another area where she was met by Inspector Lipzoni, who had a grin on her face. (It was almost as if Lauren was her ticket for a promotion.) After getting dressed, she followed the postal inspector to the back entrance of the jail and was escorted to an unmarked police car. The inspector made several attempts at small talk with Lauren, but Lauren didn't buy it and kept her mouth shut. Lipzoni was the enemy that came to her job and handcuffed her in front of everyone—and she wanted to make small talk. *I don't think so.*

They arrived at the federal courthouse where Lauren was handed over to United States Federal Marshals. They escorted her to the back of the courthouse where she sat in a small cell. One of the marshals asked her if she needed legal representation. Lauren told him that she did not. After about an hour of waiting, she was handcuffed at her hands, waist, and ankles. He then opened the cell and told her she was going before a judge. Lauren tried to walk as fast as the marshal, but it was hard for her to keep up because of her sandals. Her ankles were starting to hurt from the tightened cuffs that were rubbing against her skin. With each step that she took, the pain increased and her ankles began to swell.

They finally arrived at the courtroom. She saw her mom and sister sitting in the front row, directly behind her attorney who was sitting at a table. The minute they saw her they began to cry. It hurt them so badly to see Lauren that way. Lauren maintained her composure and smiled at them. When she reached the table where her attorney was sitting, the US Marshals removed the handcuffs from her. Lauren could not believe she was in court, it seemed like something from a movie. Sitting directly to the left of them at another table was Lipzoni and the federal prosecutor, Mandy Norwillis. Lauren saw Lipzoni take papers from her brief case and whisper in the prosecutor's ear. *I can't stand that lady.* Lauren did not like Detective Lipzoni either.

Lauren was in court to be arraigned on charges of credit card and mail fraud. After her attorney and the prosecutor went back and forth, he filed a *not guilty* plea with the court. The attorneys went back and forth for a few more minutes, and then the judge decided to let her go on her own recognizance. Lauren really didn't know what they had been discussing—all she knew was that she wanted to get out of there.

When court was adjourned, Lauren was released. Her mom and sister ran over to her right away and they began to hug each other uncontrollably. Her attorney informed them about the next steps and said that his assistant would be in touch in a few days to set up a time to meet in his office.

As they exited the courthouse, they were met by several news reporters. They shoved a microphone in Lauren's face and asked her questions about the charges. She was asked by one of the reporters why she pled not guilty. She could not believe all the commotion that was going on about her.

Lauren attempted to cover up her face as she and her sister were fighting to get through the mob of reporters. Her mother got through an opening on the side and hurried quickly to her car to get her daughters out of there. Reporters were everywhere and Lauren just could not hide. She tried to hide her face behind her sister's back to keep them from taking pictures of her. Lisa was yelling and screaming, telling them to move back and get out of the way. Once they reached the end of the steps, they could see their mother waiting in the car. They ran as quickly as they could. Once they were safely in the car, they sped away. None of them had ever faced anything like that before. They were so nervous. Lauren always wanted to be rich and famous and to be in the spotlight, but she didn't want it to happen this way.

They drove to Lauren's job—the one she had for a few hours. Her car was left there after she was arrested, so they went to pick it up and then head back to her apartment. Once there, her mom suggested that she come home for a while until everything settled down. But Lauren refused. She didn't want to leave Orlando or Jason. In fact, she still thought that, even after everything that had happened, this would all go away.

She went over to Jason's dorm that night and, for the first time, saw herself on the news—the fear of everyone finding out was now a reality. Everyone would know what she had done, including the university.

Chapter 19

LAUREN'S EXPELLED FROM COLLEGE

Soon after her arrest, Lauren received a letter from the university stating that a meeting would be held regarding her arrest and the allegations. She had the choice of having a committee of students hear her case or one faculty member. After careful decision, Lauren decided it would be in her best interest to have a faculty member hear her case, rather than the students—especially since she had used students' credit cards in her scheme.

On the day of the hearing Lauren, along with Jason for support, arrived on campus. To her surprise, Inspector Lipzoni was present by telephone and gave testimony in support of her expulsion. Lauren had never gone through an ordeal like this before and later wished she had enlisted the aid of her attorney. The week following the meeting on campus and in her final semester before graduating from college, Lauren was expelled from the university indefinitely.

The news surrounding her expulsion once again reached the news and ran non-stop in the media for weeks. The school newspaper wrote several articles about her charges and expulsion, as well as the local newspaper. The media knew everything that was going on surrounding her case. Some of things they reported were ridiculous. One news channel reported that she had been living in a yacht with three cars, while another one said she had been living in Paris at the time of her arrest. But to Lauren, none of it mattered, because people believed what they saw on the news regardless of the facts. Lauren was so humiliated and embarrassed she began to isolate herself from everyone. She had really messed up her life and she had to face the consequences of her actions.

A month after Lauren was expelled from the university she decided to enter a plea bargain in exchange for dropping one of her charges. With the possibility of facing a lengthy prison sentence, it was in her best interest to plead guilty to Possession of Stolen Mail. The charge for credit card fraud would be dropped in exchange for the plea. In addition, she was ordered to pay back over $80,000 in restitution—an amount she disputed in court. Her attorney told her there was a good chance she would not serve any time in jail—he would recommend boot camp, instead of prison. He told her that she would most likely serve her time on probation.

Inspector Lipzoni attended every single court date and was never late. She had invested a lot of time and energy on Lauren and wanted to see her case all the way through. She always had something opposing to say when it came to Lauren's freedom. She was in favor of Lauren going to prison for a long time. Lauren had not done anything to her, but assumed Lipzoni had nothing better to do with her boring life. It almost seemed as if she was fascinated with Lauren's case and rejoiced in her pain and sorrow. Lauren disliked Lipzoni with a passion. Lipzoni had her handcuffed in front of everyone, like it was a spectator sport. *I will never forgive her.*

When Lauren heard that prison might not be an option and that she might end up doing probation, she was happy. After she entered the plea bargain, her mother asked her again about coming home, but Lauren didn't want to. She wanted to stay in Orlando and ride out the storm, even though she was embarrassed and had been humiliated. As the time went on, she continued to think about suicide and wanted to end her life. But each time her attorney would bring up the possibility of probation, she would change her mind. She tried to move on with her life, but always felt like she was being watched.

One night in particular, when she and Jason were leaving the campus to get something to eat, she failed to make a complete stop at the traffic light. She was pulled over by a university police officer. She was so nervous she started shaking, Jason told her to calm down and not panic, but she couldn't help it. When the police officer approached the window, Lauren was so frantic that she told the officer who she was and that she was the lady in the news facing charges. The officer politely looked at Lauren and told her that he had no idea who she was and what she was talking about. He asked for her license, registration, and insurance. When he finished verifying Lauren's information, he told her that he had pulled her over for failing to make a complete stop at a traffic light. He issued her a ticket, told her to drive safely, and have a good night. Then he walked away. She had made a big deal out of nothing,

Later on that night, Jason told her to calm down and stop worrying, because no one knew who she was—but she wasn't buying that. In fact, her paranoia became increasingly worse such that she could hardly sleep at night. She stopped going to places in the daytime for fear of someone staring or talking about her. She stopped hanging around and visiting friends and became a hermit, secluding herself from everyone including family. She was already dealing with an issue of low self esteem; but following the aftermath of her arrest and all the media attention, she became really insecure with everyone. She knew that once this mess blew over, her life would never be the same.

Chapter 20

Lauren Loses Her Job

A few weeks after Lauren entered the guilty plea on charges of Possession of Stolen Mail, she went to pick up her check—since her arrest, she had been working at a local grocery store. When she walked in her supervisor asked to see her. She went into his office and he told her that he had a visit from the postal inspector— Lipzoni again! She had come to see him that morning. She told him that the store should be concerned about having Lauren as an employee, since she had been indicted on charges of credit card and mail fraud. She could be a huge liability to their store and may have taken customer's credit cards and used them. With this information, her supervisor decided it was in the best interest of the company to Lauren go. Lauren was shocked! She had not taken or used anybody's credit card since she left her old job in the mailroom. Now this lady was coming to her job getting her fired again. Lauren's supervisor gave her the opportunity to resign, so he didn't have to fire her. He told Lauren that he was sorry, but he had no other choice.

Lauren walked out of the store, her eyes brimming with tears. All she had left was the money in her purse from the check she had just cashed. It was December and Christmas was less than two weeks away. She felt useless and tired. She had no more energy to give, not even to herself or Jason. This would be one sad Christmas. She got in her car and drove back to her apartment. When she pulled into the parking lot, she saw a few kids getting off the school bus and began staring at them. The tears in her eyes were streaming down her cheeks and she couldn't stop them. She was crying silently in her car, like she did the night she was in the jail. She didn't want anyone to see her—and she felt safer in her car.

She just sat there and watched the kids get off the school bus. She could hear them laughing and talking to one another. They had their whole life ahead of them. They were all so innocent, like she had been when she was in high school. She wished she could magically disappear from all her madness, go back to high school, and start her life over again—but she couldn't.

She quickly wiped her face, got out of the car, and headed toward her apartment. Before she got there, she decided to get her mail. There was an envelope from the Federal Courthouse, Middle District of Florida. She was hoping it was a letter dismissing her from all charges, but she knew that wasn't the case. She opened the letter and read that the date had been set for her sentencing—in just three weeks. This was the thing she feared the most: *How much time would she have to serve on probation?*

In the weeks leading up to her sentencing, she isolated herself completely from everyone, including Jason. Their relationship had been off and on and she knew it had a lot to do with her charges and how much time she would serve on probation. He would still come around and she was happy to see him; but at the same time, she didn't expect him to stick around. He still had his whole life ahead of him and he could be with anyone he wanted.

There were a few times she wanted to go out and meet other guys, but she didn't because she wasn't a cheater—not like him. She was very faithful in their relationship and was honored to be committed to him only. She knew he messed around with other girls, she just didn't care. She believed he deserved someone better anyway—someone who wasn't facing probation time. She kept telling him that she would end up with probation and have to do community service hours; at least that is what her attorney said. At this point in her life, she just wanted the sentencing date to come and go, so she could move on with her life.

Chapter 21

LAUREN'S SENTENCING HEARING

On the morning of Tuesday, January 6, 2004 at 9:00am, Lauren reported to court for sentencing. The day had finally come when she would find out how long she would be on probation. Her mother and sister drove in the night before and Jason arrived to her apartment around eight that morning. None of them were worried because Lauren told them she was getting probation. Lauren acted as if her court date was no big deal, but deep down inside she was nervous. They drove to her attorney's office and walked over to the court house together. His office was less than a block away. Given the media frenzy that occurred the last time she was in court, her attorney decided it was best that they all walk in separately. Lauren had told Jason about the media and news reporters outside the courthouse so he would be prepared for the chaos. To their surprise, when they arrived at the front entrance, no one was there. They all walked up the stairs, entered the courthouse, went through security and walked to the elevator. They took the elevator to the room where she would be sentenced. Her attorney was talking to her mom, explaining what happens on sentencing day.

As they exited the elevator, Lauren caught a glimpse of Lipzoni. *This lady doesn't miss anything. I cannot stand her.* Lauren made up her mind that she hated Lipzoni with a passion. When they got off the elevator, they walked into another small room so her attorney could finish explaining the process. He was talking in his legal language and none of them understood anything. They were just nodding their heads and listening in unison. When he finished it was almost time for her sentencing to begin.

Lauren stood at a small table next to her attorney. She could see the prosecutor and inspector standing to the left. Once the judge entered the courtroom, they all took their seats. Before her sentencing, Lauren addressed the court and her family by reading an apology letter and accepting full responsibility for her actions. Her attorney had suggested this, saying it would show the court how remorseful she was. And then, much to her surprise, her sentencing started and was over in less than ten minutes. She was sentenced to 37 months in federal prison!

There is no way I'm going to prison. I thought I was getting probation. Lauren was dumbfounded. She had not expected a prison sentence. In addition to serving 37 months, she was required to complete a hundred and fifty community service hours and serve three years of supervised release, better known as probation.

The judge told Lauren that she would being made an example. She had committed a very serious crime and would have to pay her debt to society. He went on to tell her that he didn't care about her being in college. She would have three years to sit in prison and think about what she had done. Lauren just stood there, listening in disbelief and shock—she was going to prison.

Her attorney also stood there, not saying a word. *What happened to me getting probation?* She wanted to know about probation, because that's what he had been telling her. Her attorney was known for representing some of the worst criminal cases in town, but yet here she was being sentenced to prison. She just couldn't wrap it all around her little brain. It just didn't make any sense. He told her that he never promised her probation and that the judge sentenced her based on the sentencing guideline book. There was nothing else that could be done. He wished her and her family best of luck and then he left the room.

What about an appeal? Lauren wanted to know if she could appeal her sentence, it happened all the time on the television. But there would be no appeal for her, because she entered a plea bargain. Whenever you enter a plea, you forfeit your right to an appeal. The judge's ruling was final. *I should have paid attention in my criminal justice classes.* All she could remember was DeJohnson encouraging her to plea, so she would avoid wasting the government's time.

They were all standing there, looking at each other in complete shock. Lauren was going to prison. They hugged each other and her mom told them that everything would be alright. Yes, it was one of the worse situations they had ever encountered, but they were strong and they would get through it. Jason left the courtroom immediately after the sentencing to get the car. He figured that once Lauren's sentencing reached the news, there would probably be a lot of reporters out front—he was prepared.

Once they gathered themselves they left the courtroom. Lauren still could not believe what she just heard at sentencing; it was nothing that she and her attorney had talked about. As they were exiting the courthouse, she did her best to portray an image of self control and dignity, but it was hard. She walked out of the courthouse with her head held high—ready to face the media, her worst fear. But, to her surprise there were none, they were already gone. She found out later that the prosecutor had already talked to them, before she ever left the courthouse.

Jason pulled up. They got into the car and headed back to her apartment. The drive back was done in complete silence. Her mom attempted to make small talk, but the mood wasn't right. When they got to her apartment, her mom and sister was preparing to leave to go back to north Florida and wanted Lauren to come back with them. Again Lauren refused, telling her mom that she needed to get things in order before she went to prison. She hugged them in the parking lot, walked them over to their car, and they left.

When Jason and Lauren went inside her apartment, she tried to have a conversation with him to see how he was feeling, but Jason didn't want to talk. He didn't think there was anything left to talk about. She was going to prison for three years and that was the end of it. One of his best friends had flown into town and he wanted to go hang out with him. In her mind, she was going to prison, so she didn't even bother asking him if he was coming back or not. She decided to just leave well enough alone.

She tried to minimize her 37 month sentence, but Jason was not having it. He had already calculated her time to the three years and one month. Their relationship was already on the edge of being over and her prison sentence only added to the weight. There was nothing else she could do. She was glad everything had started to come to an end. She had told one lie after another and just didn't have the energy to waste on Jason or anyone else for that matter. If he walked out of her life at that point, it was something she would just have to deal with.

The days after the sentencing were very hard for her. She thought about committing suicide again, but never went through with it. She started smoking cigarettes and drinking beer. Her nights were long, but the days seemed even longer. She didn't have a job and no money was coming, so she was broke. She hadn't bothered looking for a job, because she knew she was going to prison. The one good friend she did have moved out of town, so they would only talk occasionally. She didn't have any money to pay her rent and would probably be receiving an eviction notice soon.

Her relationship with Jason had become really distant. She suspected him of cheating with Gina again and he was. One night she decided to go out to find his car. She was going to prison and had to see for herself. She found his car outside an apartment complex near the university. She got out of her car, walked over to his car and started pushing the alarm button. After several tries, he finally came out of the apartment. When he saw Lauren standing beside his car, he knew their relationship was over. He and Lauren were having words, when suddenly out walked Gina from the apartment. He had finally been caught. Lauren just stood there staring into his eyes, full of hurt and pain. Jason could see the hurt in her eyes and felt bad. He didn't know how she found his car, but she did. He was speechless.

Gina came down the stairs, yelling and cursing at Lauren. She told Lauren that Jason didn't want a convicted felon and that they would be getting married in a few months. Lauren was standing there, holding back the tears. When Gina reached the bottom of the stairs, she walked over to Jason caressing his back and hugging and kissing him. But his eyes never moved—they were glued on Lauren. Lauren couldn't take it anymore, she had seen enough. She took one more look at Jason and asked him why, but he never responded. She got in her car and left; their relationship was over.

She got back to her apartment and went straight to bed. She had to lie down for a moment to gather her thoughts. She couldn't believe Jason, the man she had been so dedicated to. *How could he cheat on me like this, on the day of my sentencing? He could have waited until I was in prison.* She was not the type to fuss or fight over a man. Her mother always told her that you can't make a person be with you or love you—something she finally realized. *Well, I guess he showed me who he wanted to be with.* She couldn't even cry anymore, she had no tears left. *All this time I was faithful to him, when I could have been out enjoying my time as a college student. But no, I had to go and steal some stupid credit cards just to show him how much I love him.*

She laid on her bed wondering if the judge would change his mind. *God, please change my judge's mind and not send me to prison.* But she knew his mind was not going to change and she had to do the time. She started to feel bad about what she had done. Like her judge said, she committed a crime and now she would have to face the consequences for her actions. Lauren eventually fell off asleep with prison on her mind.

Back at home, she was the topic of conversation. Somehow the local newspaper found out and had written articles about her. They knew about her being expelled from college and that her original arrest took place at her place of employment. To add insult to injury, she was getting ready to serve a three year prison sentence. All the bad things were happening to her because of her poor choices and decisions. There was nothing she could do about it now, but face the consequences. Her mom and sister were at home dealing with the embarrassment. Anytime Lisa would hear someone talk bad about her sister, she would defend Lauren. Her mom had to deal with the sly comments from customers at the bakery. Lauren's decisions had affected them as well.

But there was something that she could do that would end it all—suicide. She could do the exact same thing she did before, only this time Jason would not be there to save her. The next day Lauren got up out of bed, ready to carry out her act. She walked to her bathroom cabinet, pulled out all her bottles of pills and walked into her kitchen. Jason had half a bottle of vodka left and it would do the trick. She thought about leaving a letter, but decided not to. And just like that, Lauren took the bottle of pills and vodka. Seconds later she was on the floor, going in and out of consciousness. She wanted her life to be over.

The apartment complex had mailed out notices informing residents that they would be entering apartments to perform routine maintenance and check fire alarms. When they got to Lauren's apartment the maintenance crew knocked on her door twice, but she didn't respond. Thinking that no one was home, they entered the apartment and found Lauren on the floor— she was unresponsive. They immediately called 911 for help. A few hours later, she woke up in the hospital and learned that the maintenance crew had found her on the kitchen floor. The doctors told her that if they hadn't entered her apartment when they did, she would have died. Her suicide attempt failed again.

Her overdose incident reached the media, as did everything she did. After hearing about the incident from a teammate, Jason decided to reach out to her. They had not talked or seen each other since that night at Gina's apartment. When they talked on the phone their conversation had nothing to do with getting back together. He truly wanted to know how she was doing and to let her know that he was there for her. He really cared about Lauren and wanted to help, he just didn't know how. Hearing his voice made her feel good and happy, but she knew their relationship would never be the same.

Chapter 22

LAUREN REPORTS TO PRISON

Three weeks or so after her sentencing, Lauren received her Self Surrender Letter in the mail from the courts. She was scheduled to self surrender to the Federal Correctional Institution in Tallahassee, Florida on February 25, 2004—a day she would never forget. Lauren continued to talk with Jason, until the day she self surrendered in Tallahassee.

Her mom and sister decided to fly into town and drive Lauren's car. Her mom didn't want her car staying at the apartment. She told Lauren that she would make sure all of her things were placed in storage until her release. But Lauren wasn't thinking about a storage unit, she was heading to prison. The drive would take about eight hours to complete and they each would take turns driving. Lauren didn't want to make the drive and she didn't want to go to prison. She wanted to run away and hide forever, but she couldn't. She knew that if she didn't show up, the U.S. Marshals would be out looking for her; and she didn't want or need any more attention.

Needless to say, Lauren never did get in the driver's seat. Instead, she stayed in the back seat and took naps. She had so many chances to commit suicide; but each time she tried, someone interrupted her. *It's only 37 months. I can do that time and be home before I know it.* She tried to do everything she could to stay positive. She also couldn't help but wonder what Jason was thinking or doing. She remembered telling him the night before that she was sorry for everything that she had done to him, but she wasn't sure if he believed her or not. At any point, she realized that she had made some poor choices and decisions and the day had finally come for her to face her consequences.

They arrived at the prison around noon, but Lauren wasn't scheduled to self surrender until 1pm. When they pulled into the parking lot, Lauren's throat felt like she had a frog in it that wouldn't move up or down. Reality had set in—she was moments away from going to federal prison for three years. They sat in the parking lot for a moment. Then Lauren decided it was best to get it over with and decided to go in early. She made one last phone call to Jason and told him that she loved him. She removed her jewelry and handed it to her mother, who placed it inside the console of the car. She got out of the car and immediately felt as though the air she was breathing was about to suffocate her.

As they were walking towards the building, she couldn't take her eyes off the tall barbed wire fences. They had to be about ten feet tall or higher. She decided those fences were there to keep the inmates from escaping. The closer they walked to the building the more nervous she became. She wanted to cry and scream, but she couldn't. It was as if the frog in her throat was blocking her vocal cords from doing anything. The prison reminded her of an old college building that had been there for hundreds of years and it gave her an eerie feeling. She wanted to run in the opposite direction of the prison, but she couldn't. She was there to serve her time for the crime she had committed. *I made my bed hard and I have to lie in it.* She was getting ready to lie in her bed. She had heard all kinds of rumors about prison and how evil the people were, and she was scared to death! But there was no turning back now; she had to face the consequences for her actions.

When they entered the building, there was a correctional officer standing behind the front desk. To the right of the correctional officer, there were a couple of chairs. Her sister decided to sit down; it hurt to see her sister go to prison. Lauren identified herself to the officer and told her that she was there to self surrender. He entered her information into the computer and then told her to have a seat.

A few moments later another correctional officer appeared from the back and told Lauren to follow her. Before Lauren did, she gave her mother and sister one last hug, and then she disappeared behind another door. She followed the officer through the door. She could feel the frog in her throat and the tears falling down her face. She tried to hold back the tears, but she couldn't so the tears kept flowing. She wanted to be on the outside of the prison walls with her mom and sister.

Soon they approached a small room with a tiny cell inside of it. The officer told Lauren to have a seat in the cell while she completed the intake process. As she sat in the cell, she could still feel that frog in her throat; it wasn't going anywhere. The tears continued to flow down her cheeks and she could feel the stain on her face from the tears. It was official. She was in prison, getting ready to serve some hard time for a crime she committed. There was nowhere for her to run or hide. She had to face her consequences and she had three years to do it.

The officer could see and hear her crying and wanted to give her some encouraging words. She told Lauren that there were women in the prison serving life sentences. They would never leave there until they died, but her sentence was only three years. It would go by fast, as long as she stayed busy and didn't get into any trouble. Then she told Lauren something she would never forget. *Lauren, you're not the first person to come to the prison and you won't be the last. You're a young girl who made a mistake and you still have your whole life ahead of you. When you get out of prison, whatever you do, don't come back. It was a poor choice you made that landed you in prison, but the choices you make when you leave are more important, because they will either keep you out or bring you back.* With that being said, she went back to her desk and continued processing Lauren in.

Lauren sat in the cell wondering and thinking what her future would be like after prison. She had made a lot of mistakes in her life. And now here she was, at the age of twenty three, sitting in a Florida prison cell for the next three years. She thought about her relationship with Jason and wondered why she had allowed herself to get so caught up in him that she would commit a crime! And now she was in prison and he was a free man—he can be with whomever he pleased. Lauren knew that she had low self esteem, but she hadn't realized how bad it was until she was sitting there in the cell. The more she sat there, the more she thought about her family and how much humiliation they had suffered from her being in the media. She truly had made a huge mess of her life and there was nothing she could do about it.

About an hour or so had passed when the correctional officer came over to unlock her cell. She needed Lauren to remove all of her clothes and place them in a small brown box. Her clothes would be mailed to her mother. Once her clothes were removed, she had to be strip searched. She told Lauren to spread her legs and bend over. This would be the first of many strip searches she would endure in prison. After the search was over, she handed Lauren a pair of white underwear and brown overalls to put on, along with a pair of blue shoes and a white sack that had a towel, wash cloth, soap, tooth brush and tooth paste in it.

Next, it was picture time. She stood in front of the camera and had her picture taken. After taking her picture, she walked back to the cell. A few moments later the correctional officer handed her the prison ID with her photo on it. The card also had eight digits that read 25379-018, known as her federal prison ID number. She was told to keep her ID card on her at all times and to memorize her prison ID number, because she would be asked to say it during count time. Count time is when the officers come into the units to count the inmates to ensure that no one has escaped. The prison ID card was also important for making purchases from the commissary, which is a small store house where inmates can buy certain things on their assigned purchased day.

The correctional officer then asked Lauren if she was ready to go out into the general population or if she wanted to be in solitary. After a brief moment, Lauren said that she would be okay in general population. The officer told Lauren to gather her things and follow her—she was taking her to her unit. As Lauren was gathering her items, the frog in her throat reappeared and she started crying. Her heart began racing really fast and her hands and legs were shaking uncontrollably. Reality had set in—she was in prison.

The officer walked over towards Lauren and told her that everything would be okay. But Lauren couldn't stop crying and the tears kept coming. She told the officer that she wasn't a bad person and that she didn't mean to hurt anyone. She knew that she would have to face the consequences of her actions, but she didn't think the judge would send her to prison for three years. She was in college and was only one semester away from graduating, and now she was in prison. When Lauren stopped crying the officer looked at her and told her that she was young and had made a mistake. She went on to say to Lauren that the worst of her situation was over. She had made it through the media; now the only thing she had left to do was to complete her sentence. She then reminded Lauren again about her time and that there were plenty of women out there who would love to serve three years instead of thirty years. She told Lauren that when she finish serving her prison time, she could still go back to college, finish up her education, and become a productive member in society.

The officer took another few minutes to encourage Lauren. "Prison will either make you or break you. You made your bed hard and you will lie in it. But you will not lie in it forever. Turn your mess into a message to keep someone else from making a hard bed."

She then asked the officer if she could have a moment to say a silent prayer before going out into the general population and the officer agreed.

Chapter 23

LAUREN'S PRAYER

Lauren walked back into the cell and got down on her knees and began to pray. It was the first time she had actually acknowledged God during the entire investigation. In fact, she hadn't even bothered to pray during the time she was stealing the credit cards or even before that.

Dear God, I am sorry for what I have done and for all the people I have hurt. Please keep me safe and protected from any harm that tries to come near me. Please strengthen my mom and sister during this time. I didn't mean for anyone to get hurt, especially my family. I did commit the crime and accepted full responsibility for my actions. I am sorry. The time has come for me to pay the ultimate price, prison. Please keep my mind free and clear from anything that is not in your liking. I do not know what my future will bring, but I promise you this one thing—God, if you bring me through this, I will serve you and only you for the rest of my life. Amen.

Lauren got up off her knees, picked up her items, and walked out the door to start serving her three year prison sentence.

AUTHOR'S FINAL THOUGHTS

I wrote this book to share with everyone my story, *Consequences*. All of our actions have consequences, whether they are good or bad. The Bible says in Galatians 6:7. *Be not deceived; God is not mocked: for whatsoever a man soweth, that shall he also reap.*

During the time of this story, I did not yet have a relationship with God. Because of my wrong actions, I was put in prison—which was my consequence. God in His goodness had me in the place where He could finally get my attention. I realized I was a sinner, which separated me from God (again, my consequence). But God loved me so much that He sent His Son, Jesus Christ, to die on the cross for me. Jesus took my sin on Him, so that I could be saved. While I was in prison, I asked the Lord to be my Saviour—and He is.

After I had accepted Christ and was released from prison, I was still concerned with how others would accept or perceive me—after they found out I had been in prison. Even close family and friends were ashamed of me and would cover up my prison background by saying I was in school—when in fact I was not. There was even a time I felt the need to be comfortable in one job and not advance. I wanted to avoid having to fill out a job application and checking *yes* to the criminal background question.

The enemy wanted me to believe that my life was over; he wanted me to give up! The enemy wants us to give up. Each time we are faced with adversity, the enemy wants us—you and me—to throw in the towel and give up. In my situation, he would try and bring up my past to remind me how I used to be. For someone else, it could be something as simple as you not going to college because no one else in your family went. Or maybe even not moving forward with your business ideas because of what someone may have told you about the economy. These are just a few tactics that the enemy will use to keep us from moving forward towards our destiny. The

Bible says in John 10:10, *The thief comes only to steal and kill and destroy; I came that they may have life, and have it abundantly.* The enemy hates us! The enemy will try and use any person, situation or circumstance to alter your belief system and have you operating in FEAR and DOUBT. That is why it is important that you know the Word of God for yourself so when the enemy tries to come at you, you will be able to cast down any thought or word that is contrary to the Word of God.

For me, not only did I have to learn and study the Word of God for myself, but I had to learn how to encourage myself and speak positive in my life. Each time I said, *I can't;* God said, *You can do all things through Christ who strengthens you.* Each time the road looked hard, God said, *All things are possible to those who believe.* Each time I felt like I was all alone, God said, *I will never leave you nor forsake you.* And each time I wanted to give up, God said, *Let us not become weary in doing good, for at the proper time we will reap a harvest if we do not give up.*

The more and more I studied the Word of God, the more I realized that it is God's will that I shall have life and have it more abundantly. I started applying the Word of God in my life, and the transformation is who I am today—but know that God is not through with me yet. Granted, the transformation process hasn't been easy and it didn't always feel good. There were times I had to isolate and separate myself from people and situations. I had to accept the fact that people will judge me no matter what I did, including writing this book. Through this process, God surrounded me in the company of visionaries, leaders, motivators and believers in Christ.

I embraced my past, took responsibility for my actions, and have moved forward towards my purpose and destiny in life—you have to be willing to do the same thing. Writing *Consequences* and sharing my experiences was not easy, but I know that God will get the praise, glory and victory from it all. The enemy wanted me to operate in FEAR (False Evidence Appearing Real) and not write this book. He wanted me to be concerned about what people would say; but it didn't work, because I know who I am in Christ. And you have to be willing to do the same thing. You cannot be focused on THEM people or what THEY say. You have to set a goal, be committed, hold yourself accountable, and God will see you through. And know that if God gave you the vision, He will surely give you the provision.

So, my friend, I want to let you know, that no matter where you are in your story, you need Christ. He loves you and will accept you just the way you are, if you ask Him to. All you have to do is Accept, Believe, and Confess that Jesus is Lord and that He died on the cross for your sins, and you shall be SAVED!

In reality what you have read is just the beginning of my story. How I learned about Christ and what he has done for me is the best part. *From Inmate 2 Masters* continues my journey in prison and to Christ. Look for it in spring of 2013.

As my pastors always say, the two most important things in life are what church you go to and who you marry. Why? Because they will speak into your life every day. It is important that you surround yourself with positive and motivating people who will inspire, uplift and encourage you to be all what God has called you to be. Never allow your past, circumstances or situations keep you from reaching your purpose and destiny in life. If you have any questions about becoming a Christian and/or how to overcome adversity, please contact me: Perkins0419@gmail.com or P.O. Box 1353, Lehigh Acres, FL 33936.

God Bless,
Yolanda Flournah-Perkins
Author

About The Author

YOLANDA FLOURNAH-PERKINS was born and raised in Clewiston, Florida. After graduating from high school, she moved to Orlando to attend college. Two semesters before she was scheduled to graduate from college, she was indicted on credit card and mail fraud charges. As a result of the charges and her decisions, she was sentenced to 37 months in federal  prison. While in prison, she vowed that she would return to school and earn her degree. But even in prison, she proved to be valuable to the inmate population. She worked as a writing tutor in the education department and served as a youth mentor in a speaking group. In 2006, before she was released from prison, she gave her life to Christ.

After her release from prison, she was spent three months in a halfway house. While at the halfway house, it was challenging to find employment—she was now a convicted felon. She even met with resistant and negativity from her case manager, who told her that the only work she would ever find was cleaning up offices or working in construction. Determined to find an office job, she kept filling out applications and going on interviews until she was given an opportunity to work in human resources.

After her release from the halfway house, her next goal was to enroll in college—and she did. In 2008, she graduated *Cum Laude* with a Bachelors of Science in Criminal Justice. A week before her graduation, she married her long time partner, supporter, and boyfriend, Dwight. A condition of her release from prison was to serve three years on probation and complete 150 hours of community service—which she completed in 2009.

In 2010, Yolanda went on to further her education and earned her Masters degree. During that time she was also encouraged by her pastor to write a book. While the thought of writing a book had been an idea of hers for awhile, she had allowed fear, doubt and intimidation to rise up in her mind, and she never followed through. It wasn't until she and her husband were faced with pregnancy complications and she was placed on immediate bed rest that her pastor told her again to write. When she started to write, the enemy tried all kinds of attack on her. She experienced many pregnancy scares and was constantly in the hospital. She thought about her past and began to worry what others would think about her. But no matter the amount of attacks, her faith never wavered and she continued to speak favor and life on her unborn son. Each time the enemy tried to remind her about her past, she kept writing and thanking God for His grace and mercy.

With the support of her husband, close family, and friends, and under the spiritual leadership and guidance of her pastors, Yolanda pressed through the pain and wrote her first book,

Consequences. It is her prayer, through this book, that others will embrace their past and move forward with their purpose and destiny in Christ. By casting down the word **FEAR** (**F**alse **E**vidence **A**ppearing **R**eal) the enemy can be defeated and God's will be done.

Yolanda and her husband, Dwight, live in southwest Florida and have one son—Dwight 3rd. She is currently working on her second novel, *From Inmate 2 Masters*, scheduled to be released in the spring of 2013. She can be reached at perkins0419@gmail.com for comments, questions or speaking engagements.

CPSIA information can be obtained at www.ICGtesting.com
Printed in the USA
LVOW070803290512

283704LV00001B/3/P